WITHDRAWN
DOWNERS GROVE PUBLIC LIBRARY

Downers Grove Public Library
1050 Curtiss St.
Downers Grove, IL 60515

THE MAN
······· WITH THE ·······
GOLDEN
FLUTE

THE MAN
WITH THE
GOLDEN
FLUTE

Sir James,
a Celtic Minstrel

SIR JAMES GALWAY
with Linda Bridges

Lincoln Center

WILEY

John Wiley & Sons, Inc.

Lincoln Center and Lincoln Center for the Performing Arts names and logos are registred trademarks of Lincoln Center for the Performing Arts, Inc., in the United States and other countries. Used here by license.

Published by John Wiley & Sons, Inc., Hoboken, New Jersey
Published simultaneously in Canada

Design by Forty-five Degree Design LLC

For general information about our other products and services, please contact our Customer Care Department within the United States at (800) 762-2974, outside the United States at (317) 572-3993 or fax (317) 572-4002.

Wiley also publishes its books in a variety of electronic formats. Some content that appears in print may not be available in electronic books. For more information about Wiley products, visit our web site at www.wiley.com.

Library of Congress Cataloging-in-Publication Data:

Galway, James.
    The man with the golden flute : Sir James, a Celtic minstrel / James Galway
with   Linda Bridges.
        p.   cm.
    Includes index.
    ISBN 978-0-470-50391-1
        1. Galway, James.   2. Flute players—Biography.   I. Bridges, Linda,
    1949–   II. Title.
    ML419.G28A3 2009
    788.3'2092—dc22

    [B]

                                                                2009025213

Printed in the United States of America

10 9 8 7 6 5 4 3 2 1

To Jeanne, my favorite touring companion

Contents

· · · · · · · · · · · · · · ·

Acknowledgments

This book was inspired by my manager, Elizabeth Sobol, my long-time friend and guide. She suggested that I do this in connection with my seventieth birthday, which I am celebrating on December 8, 2009, and I thought it was a great idea if we could pull it off.

She put me in touch with Hana Lane, an editor at John Wiley & Sons. Hana is a wonderful person for getting things together. She got in touch with a writer she had worked with before, Linda Bridges, and the two of them came to visit my wife, Jeanne, and me when we were in New York last summer. We talked for a bit and decided we would go for it. But Jeanne and I were very busy, touring and teaching our annual master class. So I didn't really do much with this book until I got a series of promptings from Linda. The last of these was an e-mail that said, "Dear Jimmy, The date is fast approaching—we've got to do it." So I buckled down, and we've been e-mailing and talking back and forth ever since.

Jeanne helped me a lot, reminding me of funny things that had happened along the way, supplying names and dates, and offering me cup after cup of tea while I was working. I started to wonder,

How many cups of tea am I going to drink before we've finished this book?

I'd also like to mention Christopher McDonald, the retired former president of Rolex Japan. He also helped me by supplying dates and jogging my memory about Japan, a country that has been very important in my career.

Then there's my cousin Ann Kerr Black. Ann is one of my favorite cousins. We hadn't seen each other for a long time because of my touring schedule. But we got back in touch a few years ago, and she helped jog my memory about family members, especially my grandfather, who died when I was only four years old.

Finally, I want to say thanks to all the people mentioned in the book who helped make my life so wonderful, and to all the people who are not in the book but should have been. You cannot have a career like the one I've had without a lot of people helping you along the way, and I am very grateful to them all.

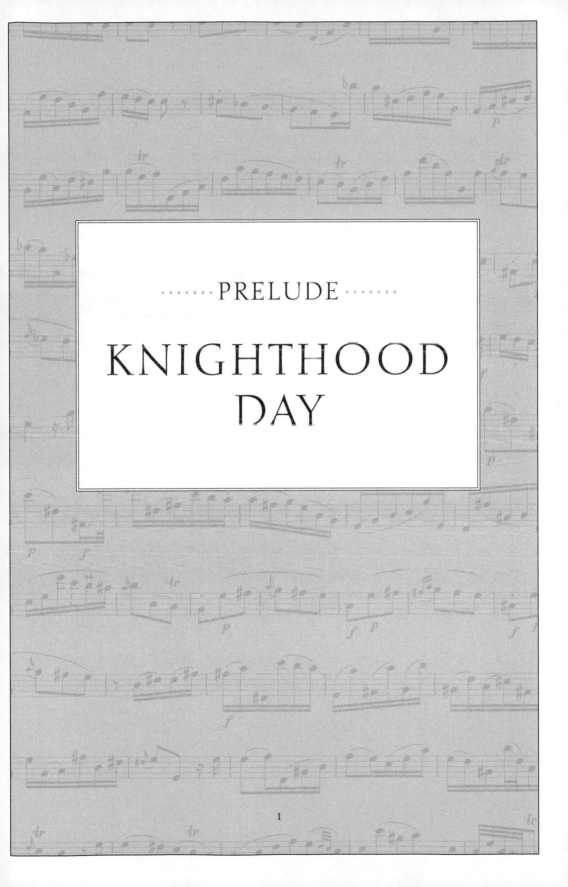

····· PRELUDE ·····

KNIGHTHOOD DAY

I T WAS THE NINTH OF DECEMBER 2001—THE DAY AFTER
my sixty-second birthday—when we all set off to London from
Switzerland, where we live. By "we," I mean my wife, Jeanne,
and my daughter Jenny and me.

The reason we were going to London was for me to receive my
knighthood from the Queen of England. That was a great occasion
in my life, but it started out not too auspiciously.

My first problem was with my British management. My name
had been on the Birthday Honours List, which comes out in June. If
your name is on the list, Buckingham Palace then gives you a choice
of dates when you can receive your knighthood. I turned this decision over to my management, but they did nothing about it. They
kept saying they wanted me to play a concert the day before or the
day after the ceremony, but they never managed to pull it together.
I believe you have twelve shots at choosing a date, and if you fail to
do so, you are off the list. So I put on my thinking cap and decided
I was not going to wait for anyone to arrange a concert for me in

order to make the trip worthwhile. At the top of my mind was the fact that this was an honor from the *queen*, and I shouldn't depend on my management to organize it for me. I simply made my own arrangements with the palace, concert or no concert.

The second problem was that my daughter Jenny has a terrible fear of flying. I find it hard to understand this from a young woman who has been flying with me since she was a small child, but there you are. When we eventually got her onto the airplane, she covered herself up from head to foot in a blanket and wasn't seen again until we landed in London. She was fine, though, once she was back down on terra firma.

Then I discovered the third problem. I had arranged with my tailor to make me a morning suit. I had told him that I was flying in just the day before the ceremony and that he should have it ready. He knows me very well, knows my measurements and everything, as I had been buying clothes from him for years. Also, he specializes in tailoring for smaller men. But when I got there, the morning suit they had for me was miles too big—it would have looked great on someone who was six foot two, which I am not. It was far too late to do anything about it. Fortunately, though, I had with me a very good Italian black lounge suit, and that was permitted. My thoughts went back to when I was nineteen years old and was going to play as an extra in the London Symphony Orchestra. I needed white tie and tails, and I borrowed them from the father of my friend Jeremy Barlow. However, by 2001 Jeremy's dad had passed away, and there was no question of borrowing a morning suit from him.

We were staying at no. 30 Chester Square, which is where I usually laid my head when in London, courtesy of my good friend Richard Colburn. We were well taken care of by Ron Young and his wife, Eileen, who looked after the house and Richard's various transient guests. On the morning of the great day, we gathered downstairs in the dining room—Jeanne in her new hat; Jenny in *her* new hat; my son Stephen, who lives in England, all spruced up; and me in my black suit.

As we were standing there, Ron, who is a Welshman with a great sense of humor, said, "Well, Sir James, give my regards to Betty."

"*Who?*" I asked.

And he said, "Betty."

"Who's that?" I asked.

"The *queen*," he said. That was his affectionate way of referring to the Queen of England.

Then our chauffeur and friend Paul Knight drove up, and we all got in the car and headed off to Buckingham Palace. There was one more hitch: when we arrived, we found that we had forgotten to bring all of the papers that were necessary to get into the palace. At first, the security guys looked at me as if I were a person from another planet, coming to the palace without our invitations and so on. However, some of the guards knew me from the various occasions when I had played there, and the others all recognized me from television—it's amazing, the power of television. They finally did let us in, and after that, all was smooth sailing.

First, I was shown to the room where we were going to rehearse the whole thing. While we were waiting, we were offered a drink and enjoyed the chitchat that precedes such an event. I met some of the other people who were receiving knighthoods that day. One of them was the chief constable of England, who was stationed in Cambridge. We got around to talking about bicycles, which are the bane of all university police.

"Don't mention bicycles to me," he said. "People steal them all the time, and it takes us hours just to write out a report for a rusty bicycle that you wouldn't take as a gift."

He added, "Once I had the bright idea of buying a hundred and fifty of them and leaving them all over the place, to see if it would alleviate the theft of students' bicycles. Of course, they were immediately stolen and painted different colors, and we never found them again."

Eventually, the palace staff collected us, and we were shown how the ceremony would proceed. We were given a lesson in how to kneel before the queen and told what would happen next.

It all rolled along to the moment of truth, and I can tell you I never thought, as my career was unfolding, that anything like this would ever happen to me. I have to confess to a touch of butterflies in my stomach, something I never experience on the concert stage. But I had no need to be nervous, because everyone at the palace was so nice and helpful; they couldn't have made it easier for us.

We were ushered to the side of the room from which we would enter the ballroom for the ceremony. I was the very first one to be called out, and I was announced to the public as "Sir James Galway." As we had been instructed, there was a little bench in front of Her Majesty. I knelt on it with my right knee, and the queen touched me on the shoulder with the beautiful dress sword of her father, King George VI, and pronounced me "Sir James."

The queen then spoke with me for a minute or two, recalling several times we had met, and she put my knighthood medallion around my neck and adjusted it just as my mother used to do with my tie when I was going to school. I thought this was very sweet.

I then went and sat with my wife and my son and daughter and watched the rest of the proceedings. The ballroom where the ceremony took place has an organ loft, and up there one of the guards' bands was playing. I'm not sure which guards they were, though, because the only way you can tell them apart is from the way the buttons on their tunics are arranged—whether they're in groups of three going down the front of the tunic, or three and then two, or two and two—and we weren't close enough to see them clearly.

In any case, they were playing away, and some of it was very funny. They played arrangements that were left over from the 1950s, and it sounded like an old radio program. Some of the music really suited the situation, though. For example, when one chap came up to receive his honor, the band launched into "The Teddy Bears' Picnic"—and the man actually *looked* like a teddy bear. I'm sure the queen had a difficult time keeping a straight face.

When all of the honors had been awarded, we were taken outdoors to be photographed. While we were doing this, I saw two

Here we all are after the ceremony—my daughter Jenny, me, my wife, Jeanne (on her first day as Lady Galway), and my son Stephen—with my knighthood medallion front and center.

yeomen. I had always wanted to have my picture taken with the Yeomen of the Guard. By the way, it was freezing cold—freezing like you wouldn't believe. But I asked these two chaps whether I could have a picture taken with them, and they said, "Of course." One of them—without looking at me; he was looking straight ahead—said, "Sir James, I bought a tin whistle."

To which I replied, "Are you trying to get divorced?"

And he said, "Well, I *have* been practicing it a lot, but my wife doesn't mind." I thought this was rather funny—everywhere I go, somebody tells me he is playing the flute or the tin whistle.

All in all, this was one of the greatest days in my career—in my life, in fact. I felt as if I'd been put in a different category: I was no longer Mr. Galway; I was Sir James. An honor of this sort is not like a doctorate, for example. It signifies that my entire life's work, all of my services to music, have been recognized by the British Crown.

There was a practical effect, too. I soon discovered that the queen, by giving me this title, had taken me from the hardworking class and put me into the super-hardworking class. Suddenly, everyone wanted to have my name on something or another. I always try to oblige for anything I believe is a good cause, because these organizations need any bit of help you can give them.

Anyhow, that was The Day, and it brings me back to where it all started: in Belfast, at the beginning of World War II.

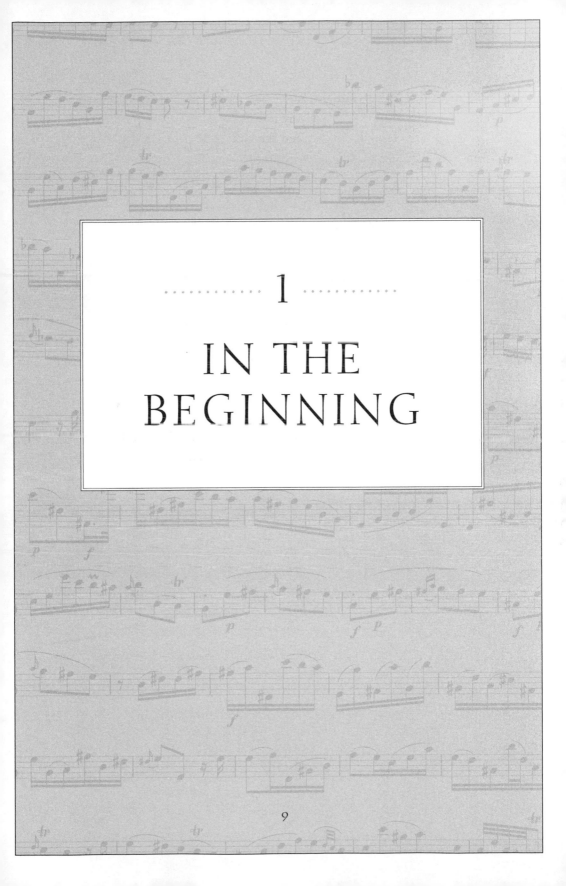

1
IN THE BEGINNING

THE FLUTE WAS IN MY BLOOD, YOU MIGHT SAY. My grandfather, also named James Galway, was a highly regarded flute player in Belfast. He in turn taught my father—another James Galway—to play the flute, which he did very well. So as small children my younger brother, George, and I grew up to the sound of the flute.

Our grandfather came to live with us during the last years of his life. He didn't socialize much with us boys, or tell us stories about the old days. But in the evenings, after George and I had been sent upstairs to bed, he often played softly for a while, a few tunes he was especially fond of. I loved listening to him, and I held off falling asleep as long as he was playing. My father, meanwhile, was devoted to Mozart. By the time I was eight, I could recognize the main themes of Mozart's G Minor Symphony and *Jupiter* Symphony, because my father played them for me over and over.

Although my grandfather was self-taught, he was good enough that he had often played in the opera orchestra. But his real passion was playing in the flute bands that we had in Belfast. These bands were the equivalent of marching bands in the United States, or the brass bands they had up in the north of England. The flute bands played traditional Irish tunes in parades—many of them Orangemen's tunes, I should add, because most of the flute bands were Protestant. But they also gave concerts where they played classical music, if you can imagine playing an overture arranged for thirty-two flutes, four drums, a bass drum, cymbals, and triangles.

My grandfather was the conductor of one of the best bands in Belfast, called the Apprentice Boys, which regularly won the local competitions. In fact, they were the champions right up to World War II. My father was also a member of the Apprentice Boys. But to my great regret, I never had a chance to hear their band play. I was born just three months after the beginning of World War II, on December 8, 1939, so I wasn't even two years old when Adolf dropped a bomb on the Apprentice Boys' humble music-making abode and demolished it. They never recovered from that. They never found a new home after the war or even got together to play again.

For that matter, Adolf also bombed our first house, on Vere Street, and we had to move around a bit before settling in at no. 17 Carnalea Street. The problem was that our neighborhood was cheek by jowl with the shipyards, a part of Belfast that was a prime target of the Luftwaffe. Shipbuilding and shipping had been the big industries in Belfast, which had one of the largest dry docks in the world. In fact, the *Titanic* had been built in Belfast. My grandfather might even have worked on the *Titanic*, although we don't have any evidence of that.

Anyway, this was industrial Belfast, and in the winter we had fogs where you couldn't see a thing. You've heard of the "London particulars"—well, they had nothing on our Belfast fogs. I presume that half of the *Titanic* was built in the dark, because these fogs were so bad. They lingered all the way up to the sixties, when the British government finally forbade burning coal. Smokeless fuel was the order of the day, and all of a sudden we could see.

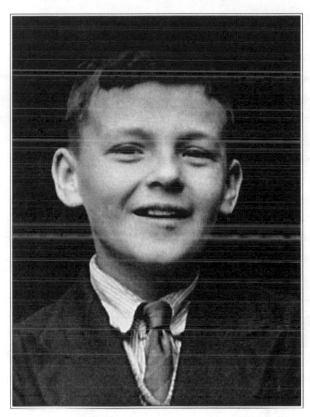

When I was a very young lad, just nine years old.

My parents and my grandparents and their friends were in the lower working class—not that they could always get work. Shipbuilding fell off after World War II, and my father was often unemployed, although he did pick up a nice bit of money playing the accordion in dance bands. My mother was the main breadwinner in the family, working as a winder in a spinning mill. She was also a keen amateur musician. She played the piano, entirely by ear—she had never learned to read music or wanted to. But if she heard a tune, she could play it, and she was a great favorite playing for women's guilds and other groups.

We didn't have a lot of money or special clothes—a nice suit was reserved for going to church on Sunday and for weddings and funerals. Otherwise, people basically lived in the same clothes that they wore to work or school. But we always had a roof over our heads, except when the Luftwaffe bombed us, and I don't remember ever going hungry, although there were times when we didn't have much besides bread and butter.

We lived in a neighborhood that was built by the people who owned the shipyards to house their workers. Like most of the houses on our street, ours had two rooms upstairs, and downstairs a kitchen, a little back room, and a sitting room. There was no toilet—just an outhouse in the backyard. And no bathtub. We used the same tub that my mother washed clothes in, and we had a bath every Saturday night. If it was cold, the tub was set up in front of the fire.

The idea behind the Saturday bath was to get ready to go to church on Sunday. In fact, my parents didn't go to church regularly, although if anyone had asked them, they certainly would have said they were Protestants. But at some point I started going to church. At first I tried the church on the corner, St. Paul's, which was next door to the primary school that George and I went to. But I found I didn't much like St. Paul's. It was Church of Ireland—that is, Anglican—and I felt that the ministers and many of the parishioners talked down to people like me. You know, they had a posh accent, and because we had real Belfast street accents, we didn't seem

With my mum and my brother, George, at our home on Carnalea Street. That's George on the left, me on the right.

to fit in. So I found another church, down by the docks, where they seemed to be sort of normal people. And I enjoyed that. It was a Presbyterian church called Sinclair Seamen's Church.

I went back to this church much later, one time when I was visiting Belfast, and it was just the way I remembered it from childhood. The leaded windows portrayed soldiers and sailors, the pulpit looked like the prow of a ship, and there was a lot of ship paraphernalia, including a big ship's bell, which had been recovered from a bad accident at sea. Sinclair Seamen's is still there, I'm glad to say, and seems to be doing very well.

At that time, nobody in our neighborhood had a TV. We just had radios, and our radio was pretty bad. It was likely to break down at the worst possible moment. You'd be in the middle of a heavyweight championship fight, and the announcer was describing how there was a left to the head, a right to the body, and Joe Louis was down again—and then the radio would cut out. But the other side of it was that we listened to a lot of music. As a kid, I used to get the *Radio Times*, which was the official guide to the BBC. I always looked up the classical-music bits on the Third Programme, and I heard a lot of wonderful music for free.

Not that my life was all high-toned and classical music. I used to tool around the town with a few of my mates, and we got up to all sorts of devilment. For starters, there were the trams. The fathers of some of my friends were tram drivers, and we waited until one of their trams came along and then all piled onto it, free of charge. You can't imagine what ruffians we were. But the drivers got a kick out of it, and from our parents' point of view, if a bunch of ten-year-olds went into town on a neighbor's tram, he sort of kept an eye on you. Of course, once we got off the tram, the city was our oyster.

Then there was the railway station. It was very near Carnalea Street—you could see it from the next corner, and you could walk there in two minutes. Now, the station was just one amazing place for us to play in. We ran all over it and got into things, and the porters would yell at us and chase us away. I realized later that it was in fact quite dangerous, as there was quite a bit of shunting of goods in the areas where we played. But I don't remember anyone ever getting hurt, and it was great sport.

It was quite a while after the war before lorries began to make deliveries from the railway station. When we were kids, they still used horses and carts—huge dray horses pulling the carts. We would go over and ask the guys who were going out on a run if we could come with them. They seemed delighted to have some kids along, keeping them company. They got us to do a bit of work for them as well—when they made a delivery, we helped them unload the things. Then they brought us back to the railway station. And this way we got to know Belfast a little, because they delivered to shops all over town.

Meanwhile, ever since we were youngsters, my brother and I had been fascinated by Dad's flute. We were constantly getting at it and trying to play it. He tried to hide it, but our house wasn't very big and we were very determined. So then he started taking it apart and hiding the pieces separately, but that only made it more of a game. Finally, to keep me away from his flute, he bought me my first musical instrument—a mouth organ. Only there was something wrong with it—I couldn't make the sounds that I wanted to. It turned out that it had only whole tones, not half tones, which meant that you could only play in the key of C major. So he found me another one that cost £2 and had a button on the side that let you play half tones as well, and then I was happy. I could play "White Christmas" and "Rudolph, the Red-Nosed Reindeer" and cowboy tunes like "Old Smokey" that we'd heard Gene Autry and Roy Rogers sing in the movies on Saturdays.

But I never gave up hankering for the flute, and finally my father got me one. It was nothing like the classical Boehm-system flutes I graduated to only a couple of years later—the kind used in professional orchestras. No, this one was a simple six-key instrument of the kind used in military bands, which is what most of the Belfast flute bands used.

Back then, I often wondered what the future would hold, and one day something very odd happened. I was at home with my mother, and we heard a loud knock on the door. Mum opened it, with me standing right behind her, and there was an old gypsy woman. She handed my mother a sprig of heather, but then she wanted to talk. Mum didn't invite her in but didn't close the door either. After a few minutes of chatting, the gypsy woman looked at me and asked me to let her see my hand. I thrust it out to her. She studied my palm and said, "You know, one day you're going to be a great musician."

I didn't believe that she could really tell the future. Yet those words stayed with me and may have had something to do with strengthening my desire to make music my life's work.

Around the age of nine, I was given a violin by Mrs. Shearer, who lived up the street from us, and I began to take lessons with a friend of my father's, Richard McKay, or "Wee Dickie," as we all called him. This was not a great success. In the first place, the violin was home sweet home to an army of Irish woodworms. Once I became familiar with the tiny holes where they lived, I realized they were eating up the whole house. Another problem I had was that my eyes were very poor when I was young, and the music for the violin has to be much farther away than for the flute. Well, it was a great day for the Irish worms when I abandoned the violin, and they could chomp away without my providing the music for their dinner. I had never stopped playing the flute, and now I went back to it full-time.

Somehow, when I was about ten and playing the flute not too badly, my father had the chance to buy me a more serious flute—a Selmer Gold Seal—for £21. That was an amazing amount of money, because even when he was working he earned only £4 a week. How he managed to scrimp and save to get this flute, I will never know, but I was very grateful for it. Unfortunately, the instrument had something wrong with it, and it did not improve with my efforts to fix it.

After a few months, I took it around to a man named Purdy Flack, who repaired instruments in his home. He looked it over and said, "I don't think this is much good. But I have something here I think would suit you. Tell your dad it's only thirty pounds." That would be the equivalent of more than $2,500 today.

My father almost died, but he had me play the flute for him, and he realized this was something that might really make a difference for me. So he somehow came up with the money again.

Now that I had a proper flute, all I wanted to do was play it. The problem was that I wanted to play tunes. Like my mother, I could pretty much hear a tune once and then play it. But my father believed that if you were going to learn properly, you had to practice your scales, and you even had to learn some theory—which he had managed to teach himself, without any formal studies. On the first score, I eventually realized that he was right; on the second, I had my doubts—and I still think music schools spend too much time on theory for students who are learning to be singers or instrumentalists, as opposed to composers or arrangers.

Because my father had quite a temper, there were plenty of rows between us. I wanted to play "White Christmas" or "South of the Border" or some of the great marches, like "Men of Harlech" or an Orangemen's tune called "The Sash My Father Wore." Dad wanted me to practice my scales. One time I went up to my room and was playing "Men of Harlech" in the key of A major, and I was having trouble with a G-sharp. Dad came tearing up the stairs and burst into the bedroom, yelling, "There, you see! If you'd learned the scale of A major properly, you'd be able to play that." Anyway, after a while my father decided that we weren't getting anywhere this way, and so he sent me off to Uncle Joe for lessons. Uncle Joe wasn't really my uncle—he was actually a second cousin, and his full name was Joseph McAdorey—but that's what I always called him. He was the bandmaster of the Onward Flute Band, and he was a great guy. He lived with his mother, who was my grandfather's niece, but we all called her Granny Mac. She wore a black shawl, and she had her silver hair in a bun in the back. Her hair was very long—I remember once seeing it before she wound it up in the bun, and I was amazed at how long it was.

Granny Mac always had Joe's supper ready as soon as he came home from work, and I arrived with my flute not much later. After Joe had eaten and spent a few minutes chatting with his pet canary, he would turn to me: "Okay, young fellow, get your flute out."

So I would prop up my music and ask him to sing the piece to me and then to play it on the flute. I've always found this to be the best way to learn a piece of music: have someone else play it, or listen to a good recording—and then try to do it better.

Anyway, I thought the world of Uncle Joe's flute playing. Most of the players in the Belfast flute bands had a sluggish approach, but he had a clean, crisp way of attacking the notes that appealed to me very much. I learned a lot from his way of playing.

He was also very good at teaching the basics. Unlike Dad, he didn't discourage me from playing marches and songs from the movies. He even taught me another song, "Children's Love," that I'm still fond of. So I didn't resent it when he made me practice my scales or count out a piece before I ever put the flute to my lips, to get the rhythm right. I remember the first time I tried to play something in 6/8, I just *couldn't* get it right. It was one of the most frustrating experiences of my nine-year-old life. But finally, with Uncle Joe's help—and spurred on by his promise that when I was good enough, I could join his band—I managed to play the piece.

Another thing Joe insisted on was learning to read music. It was all well and good, he said, to pick up tunes by ear, but being able to read the music would open up a lot more possibilities. So, one way and another, even though much of it was hard, tedious work, I enjoyed my lessons and my practicing.

When I was about ten, Uncle Joe did take me into the Onward Flute Band, and I thought that was the greatest, because it gave me a sense of belonging to something. We met every Tuesday and Friday evening in our practice room above a barbershop, and I was the youngest one there by a good bit. We had sixteen flutes, a bass drum, a couple of other drums, triangles, and a cymbal, and you can't imagine how all of that sounded in our little practice room. One time I complained to Uncle Joe, "I can't hear myself playing at all."

"That's good," Joe explained. "That means you're in tune—everybody's in tune. You can only hear yourself if you're out of tune."

Not long after I joined the band, we entered the annual Flute Band League competition held at the Ulster Hall, a big deal indeed in the Belfast flute world. We had a particular piece to play called "Silent Valley," and I practiced that piece as if my life depended on it. I had never been shy about playing in front of people, but this was the first time I had sat on a stage and looked out at a packed house. Our turn came pretty early in the evening, and I believed we had done well, but we had quite a while to wait before finding out what the judge thought. So we went to a nearby pub for part of the time, and I drank Coke while my dad and the fellows in the band mostly drank other things. At some point, we had dinner at a fish-and-chips place and then went back to the hall. It was after midnight when the last band finished playing, whereupon the judge emerged from his little box and announced that the winner was the Onward. I was beside myself with joy.

Although competitions were important to the flute bands, their real raison d'être was to march through the streets on special occasions. The Onward members wore dark-blue uniforms with red trim, and we each had a little music holder that fastened onto the left arm. I thought that marching through the streets in my uniform, playing away, was the greatest thing in the world, especially if some of my friends were standing along the parade route and called out, "Hey, Jimmy," as we went by.

The really big deal was "the Twalth," to give it the local pronunciation—the Twelfth of July, when the Ulster Orange lodges celebrate the victory of the Protestant William of Orange over the Catholic King James II at the Battle of the Boyne. All the Orange lodges, as well as the bands, march in the parade. Before the war, my dad would have marched with the Apprentice Boys, but after they broke up, he didn't join another band. So by the time I was in the Onward, he marched with his lodge, the Imperial Temperance 929—which may sound a little funny, given that temperance wasn't exactly his style.

In any case, early on the morning of the Twalth, all the bands and the lodges gathered at Carlisle Circus and, led by the grand master, got set to walk the twelve miles to the Field of Finaghy. There the speeches went on forever, and I found them intensely boring. I really had no interest in politics—I still don't—and one problem with Ulster Protestants is their tendency to believe you mustn't enjoy yourself, lest you get up to the Pearly Gates and St. Peter tells you, "No, you're not coming in here, my lad." But during the three years I marched on the Twalth, I usually managed to have some fun at the Field—eating and maybe dancing a bit on the grass and getting a chance to try blowing other instruments.

The icing on the cake was that we actually got paid for this. I remember one time I was paid £35—an amazing sum for us in those days. I bought a bicycle with it, and that was the pride of my life until somebody stole it.

One day I was walking along High Street with a couple of my mates, and we came across a sign that read, "Atlantic Records." We went inside; the room was only a little cubbyhole with no windows underneath a big staircase. But there was enough space for Solly Lipschitz to have his shop and to conduct the business of selling records. He was rightly known as Solomon Lipschitz, but everyone called him Solly.

Now, we boys all looked like the hero of *Angela's Ashes* and were reckoned by the local shopkeepers to be up to no good. But Solly took one look at us and said, "What instruments do you fellows play?" Because everybody around there played something.

We said, "We play the flute."

"Okay," he said, "you play the flute. Well, let's see what we have." He hunted for a record and put it on the gramophone. It was the Berlin Philharmonic, he told us, conducted by Wilhelm Furtwängler. They were playing variations by Hindemith on a theme of Weber's. The piece has an impressive flute solo, and when the record reached the solo, we were all listening. Afterward, Solly asked, "What do you think, fellows?"

We all gave it the thumbs-down. In the Belfast flute-band tradition, we were letting on that if it wasn't in 2/4, and it wasn't called "Old Comrades" or "Under the Double Eagle," it didn't fall into our notion of what flute music was supposed to be.

"*What?*" Solly exclaimed. "This is the Berlin Philharmonic, and it's Furtwängler conducting!"

And we said, "We don't care—we don't like the flute player. Can you play us a march?"

Well, Solly didn't give up on us, and we went there every Saturday. He usually played us several records, and we had a wonderful time. In fact, he educated us as far as classical orchestral music goes.

Only years later did I realize that Solly was Jewish. It never crossed my mind at the time that anybody in Belfast would be Jewish. In Belfast, I thought, we had Protestants and Catholics; Jews existed only in the Old Testament and the New Testament. Solly was very proud when he heard I had got the solo flute job in the Berlin Philharmonic, in spite of what I had said about that orchestra in the innocence of youth.

. . . .

Although Uncle Joe had done a good job of getting me started on the flute, my dad thought it was time to send me to a more professional teacher. He had a friend named Ardwell Dunning, a bookbinder by trade but also a fine flute player. He was a dapper little man, past seventy when he first started teaching me, but one of the finest teachers I have ever had, and that's saying a lot.

Uncle Joe had taught me to be rigorous about counting and had made me practice my scales. Now Artie introduced me to harmony and explained how understanding harmony would help me play the notes accurately. He also let me play his beautiful Boehm-system flute, which made the time that we spent doing the exercises in *Steiner's Harmony* less painful. He was always very encouraging to his young pupil. One time I said to him, "Look, Artie, why is it everybody else can play the flute louder than I can?"

He answered, "You know, Jimmy, you're just a small boy. All these other chaps you play with are grown up; they're big and strong. I can only tell you that one day when you're big enough, you too will be able to play as loud as you want." Well, like my father, I never did get to be very big—but big enough, at least, to fulfill Artie's promise.

I loved Uncle Joe, but as my playing improved, I yearned for bigger things than the Onward, so when I was about eleven I joined the Belfast Military Band. This band didn't stick to flutes and percussion: it had trumpets, cornets, clarinets, bassoons, and even E-flat euphoniums. Soon after I joined this band, a military-band competition was to be held in the Ulster Hall. The test piece was the *Coppélia Suite* by Délibes, which has a wonderful piccolo solo. I had never played the piccolo before I started to learn this piece. Although it's smaller than the flute and therefore has smaller finger holes and keys, it's played pretty much the same way. I worked and worked on my part, afraid that I would let down my new bandmates. But on the evening of the competition, our performance went perfectly, and to my joy and theirs, we won.

My next competition was something else again. It was called the Irish Flute Band Championships, and there were three classes for soloists: one for ages ten to thirteen, the "junior class" for ages thirteen to sixteen, and the open class. Well, having a pretty good opinion of my playing after the previous competition, I entered all three classes.

The competition had three set pieces: an arrangement of an aria from Donizetti's opera *La Favorita*; Anton Rubinstein's "Melody in F," originally written for the piano; and a Viennese song called "Schön Rosmarin," written by Fritz Kreisler for the violin. Uncle Joe helped me with the rhythms of the Donizetti. At first, I found the Rubinstein the most difficult, but after I listened to the Palm Court orchestra play it a few times on the BBC, it started to fall into place. And I got hold of Kreisler's own recording of "Schön Rosmarin." But in that case listening wasn't enough: the Viennese style was just too foreign to me. Fortunately, the father of a friend of mine, Billy Dunwoody, was able to help me get into it.

When the evening of the competition arrived, my father took me on the bus to St. Anne's School near Sandy Row, just a few minutes' ride from our house. We went upstairs to the third floor, where a large classroom had a platform that served as the stage. It turned out that there were ten players in each class, and we were given numbers that were then put in a hat for a drawing to determine what order we would play in. The judge, who sat in a sort of box on the stage from which he could hear but not see the players, was not given the names that went with the numbers until after he had finished judging us.

It may be hard to imagine nowadays, but most of the people in the audience were puffing away on cigarettes. By the time Dad and I arrived, the atmosphere in the classroom was nearly as thick as a Belfast fog. Each time my number was called, though, I managed to find my way to the stage and play my piece.

The competition started at seven thirty and didn't finish until after midnight. The judge didn't announce the results of each class when it was over; instead, he stayed in his box until everyone had played. When he finally emerged, he first mumbled a few words about the "fine playing" he had heard, then for each class he read off the names, starting at the bottom of the rankings, and gave the score for each. I remember my score in the soloists-aged-ten-to-thirteen class: 96½. Then the judge formally announced the third, second, and first prize winners, and first prize was James Galway. I went up to the stage and was given a little cup.

The same routine was repeated for the junior class, and once again it was "first prize, James Galway." So I went up to the stage and collected a second cup, this one a bit bigger.

Then the judge came to the open class—and yet again it was "first prize, James Galway." The house erupted, and the judge looked as if he couldn't believe the same player—and an eleven-year-old boy at that—had won all three classes. But he handed me my third cup. I dashed home with my dad and said, "Look, Mum, look at these!" and we put them up on the mantelpiece. My parents didn't fuss over me too much, not wanting me to get a swelled head. But up until then, whenever Dad called out to me, it would be, "Hey, big fellow!" After that night, it was, "Hey, Mozart!"

I was on the brink of a change in direction whose importance I wouldn't fully realize for years to come. By this time, I had joined another flute band, the 39th Old Boys. My best friends there were Billy Dunwoody, whose father had helped me prepare for the competition, and another fellow named Edmund Duke. Edmund was a brilliant flute player, and there were many other fine players in the 39th: Billy Drennan, an excellent bass drummer, and his two talented children, Joyce, a trumpeter, and Jim, a pianist. And Ray Stevenson, the brother of one of my teachers at the Mountcollyer school, was a fine flute player.

I loved playing with the 39th and didn't have any higher aspirations than that, but Billy and Edmund gave me some advice that changed my life. They told me of a woman named Muriel Dawn, a flutist with the BBC orchestra in Belfast, who had a remarkable technique. Mrs. Dawn also took pupils, and both Billy and Edmund said that if I could possibly manage it, I should study with her.

I badgered my father, and he finally called her up and made an appointment for the following Sunday. Mrs. Dawn lived in a rather grand suburb, Cherryvalley, which my father and I set out for on the appointed day. Of course, we got lost. We wandered around for quite a while and were two hours late by the time we finally found her house. Dad apologized, but Mrs. Dawn, a very impressive lady with a cap of snow-white hair, merely said, "Oh, never mind; let's have a cup of tea and talk things over."

We did that, and I found her very appealing, but no commitment was made either way. Much later, she told me about the conversation that ensued between her and her husband, Douglas. As she related it to me, he said, "What about teaching him?" and she retorted, "What's the point— teach him to play in a flute band? But where does he go afterward? There's nothing he can do except play better than the other people in the flute band."

Yet I kept phoning her to ask, "Are you going to teach me?" And finally she agreed.

I eventually learned that she and Douglas were English; they came from Sheffield, in Yorkshire. They had both had fine musical careers in England, he as a pianist and clarinetist, she as a flutist and singer. In fact, she had sung some of Ralph Vaughan Williams's songs with the composer as her accompanist. She had also sung with the Queen's Hall Orchestra conducted by Sir Henry Wood—the original conductor of the Promenade Concerts in London. But at some point, the Dawns had decided to move to Northern Ireland. As I've mentioned, Muriel played with the BBC orchestra, and in 1951, just about the time I met them, Douglas was appointed musical adviser to the Belfast Education Committee. Soon afterward he founded

I owe more than I can ever repay to my beloved flute teacher Muriel Dawn.

the Belfast Youth Orchestra, which gave a start to many musicians who went on to fine careers throughout the United Kingdom.

In any case, I was eleven when I began going to Cherryvalley, out in southeastern Belfast, every Saturday with my flute and my seven and sixpence (which seemed like a great deal of money to the Galways but was only the equivalent of about $30 today).

The first lesson was quite a comedown for this lad, who had never lost a competition, even against grown men who were far more experienced players. Muriel started by asking me to play a piece for her. When I finished, instead of complimenting me on how well I played, she said, "Now, Jimmy, you've got to learn the basic method of blowing the flute." She paused and then added, "We must now lay a groundwork that will last you forever. So for the next month, I don't want you to play the flute at all, merely the headpiece." And sure enough, for the next month she made me work on nothing but the embouchure—the way you hold your lips to control the flow of air into the flute. It nearly killed me, having to do this for twenty minutes every day, but I must have trusted her even then because I did as she said. Of course, when nobody was watching I would secretly play the flute. But this special training in the embouchure is something that has stayed with me all my life. Once I understood it, I could adjust it as the years went by and my physical makeup changed.

Finally, Muriel let me put the flute back together, but I still wasn't allowed to play tunes. At first, she had me playing only one note, holding it as long as I could, then varying the dynamics—making it louder and softer. Next, she had me buy a book by Marcel Moyse, the great French flutist. Her teacher Geoffrey Gilbert had learned from a French teacher, and this tradition was handed down to her. Indeed, when Billy and Edmund had told me about her, they said her playing was in the style of Moyse. This book is called *De la Sonorité*, and it has a number of exercises that help the student control the tone and the dynamics, so that I started to learn how to play a low note loudly and a high note softly, two of the harder things to do on the flute. When I left for England four years later, Muriel warned me, "Now, whatever you do, don't let anybody change your embouchure and don't let anybody change your system."

Douglas Dawn also played an important role in my training. I was a charter member, you might say, of his Belfast Youth Orchestra, the first orchestra—as opposed to a band—that I'd ever played with. Through no fault of Duggie's, it wasn't much of an orchestra in its early days, although it later became a very fine one—one of the best youth orchestras in the United Kingdom. But for those first rehearsals, we had, as I wrote in an appreciation of Duggie after his death, "about 12 flutes, 8 clarinets, 2½ oboes, 1 cello, 1 viola, and a few violins." And most of the string players seemed to be tone-deaf, judging by the sound of their playing. Still, we didn't do too badly in our first concert, at which we played Beethoven's Fifth and Handel's "Where'er You Walk," which has a wonderful flute solo.

Muriel was my teacher, but Douglas gave me some very helpful coaching. He had a tight hand with young players—he wouldn't let you stray too far from what the composer had written. But he did leave room for you to express your own personality as well. And he never phrased his criticism unkindly. I remember once when I was playing the minuet from Bizet's *L'Arlésienne* suite, and Duggie interrupted me: "No, look! This note has to sound very nice and easy. We don't want it to sound too loud but nice and controlled and soft." Of course, he was right. I never imagined that day that the next time I would play that little minuet would be in a recording with the Berlin Philharmonic under Herbert von Karajan.

Douglas and Muriel went out of their way to open my eyes and ears to new things. Whenever I was first learning a piece, Douglas always played me a recording of it by a first-rate artist, and he and Muriel both encouraged me to listen to the Promenade Concerts on the BBC, which my father and I gladly did. The Dawns also took me to museums to introduce me to great paintings. For that matter, their own drawing room was like nothing I had ever seen, with many beautiful canvases by Irish painters.

Most important, they took me to concerts, especially those by the British Music Society. Much later, after I had gone out into the world and had begun to make my way as a soloist, Muriel wrote to me: "Right at the beginning, the way you appreciated the phrasing and shaping was astonishing; as was the way you appreciated the best from the not-quite-so-good. It was built into you—not something you acquired. You brought *feeling* with you right from the beginning—it never had to be put into you. You know, with some of the singers I teach, you have to go inside and struggle to get them to release what's there. There was never that trouble with you."

Meanwhile, I had to think about getting a job. I was coming up to school-leaving age, which in those days was fifteen if you weren't preparing to go to university. Even if I hadn't had to contribute to the family exchequer, continuing in school wouldn't have been my choice. I had liked some of the teachers a lot, especially our English teacher, David Honeyman; our form teacher, James Stephenson, whom we affectionately called "Stabo"; and our social studies teacher, Malcolm McKeown.

But what I remember about Malcolm isn't what he taught us about social studies; it's his musical side. He was a very fine tenor and performed around town in various musical events. He also sang in things like the Bach B Minor Mass with the local amateur orchestra. I played fourth flute with the orchestra, wearing my school uniform while everyone else wore black tie. Our budget at home did not run to a dinner jacket and black tie. Fortunately, the people running the concerts made allowances for the Galway household budget.

One day Malcolm heard me playing the flute during a break. He wanted to know what the piece was, and when I told him, he asked, "Is there a piano part?" I said, "Yes, there is." The next day I brought the music to school, and he played the piano for me. Now, this was a big mistake on his part. Every day at lunchtime I would come looking for him, and he never got a minute's peace. It was wonderful for me, though. We played Bach sonatas and that sort of thing. After he retired, he moved to England. Some years later, I visited him once, and he served me some very fine Scotch. That was the last time I saw dear Malcolm.

One thing I had loved in school was learning bookbinding. By the time I was fourteen, I had produced some leather-bound books that were really beautiful. But when I applied for a job with a bookbinding firm, they passed me by. I was terribly disappointed, because this was something I really wanted to do. Despite all that the Dawns had done for me, it still hadn't occurred to me that I could ever make my living as a professional musician.

Then Duggie told me there was an apprenticeship available with a firm that made and reconditioned pianos. I applied for it, and this time I was accepted. I went to work there for twenty-three shillings a week (about $80 today). The idea was that the apprentices would learn to repair and tune pianos, while doing various menial jobs in the meantime. So we sanded and buffed the keys and removed and replaced strings. Those were the better jobs; the one I really hated was cleaning out glue pots. To make matters worse, the tuners liked to keep us boys in our place, and the foreman was a petty tyrant. But at least the owner, Thomas Tughan, was a kind and decent man.

Whenever I wasn't working, I played the flute. One day Duggie said, "Jim, we'll have to get you into the Philharmonic"—meaning the Belfast Philharmonic. Well, the Phil accepted me, and I played with it for a little while, but I didn't care for its repertoire. I remember that we played some Elgar, *The Dream of Gerontius*, and it really wasn't for me.

But then a local BBC producer and conductor named Havelock Nelson invited me to join his orchestra, a semiprofessional group called the Studio String Orchestra. Despite its name, it had a woodwind section, and I got to play second flute to my idol at the time, Edmund Duke. This was more my cup of tea. I remember playing *St. Matthew Passion* with the Studio Strings, and it was first-rate. And this is when I took part in my first BBC broadcasts.

I was still playing with the 39th Old Boys—in fact, I stayed with them until I left Belfast for London. Meanwhile, my chums Billy Dunwoody and Edmund Duke and I formed a trio—the Zephyr Trio, we called it—and we staged a few concerts. Duggie helped us shape our repertoire, and he also accompanied us. I remember that at one of our concerts, he accompanied me in the rather flashy "Concertino" by Cécile Chaminade. I was amazed at how many of our neighbors turned up to hear that concert.

So, you might say I had a pretty busy schedule for a fifteen-year-old—Tuesday and Friday evenings with the Old Boys, Wednesday evenings with the Studio Strings, and Saturday evenings with the Youth Orchestra; plus my regular Saturday lesson with Muriel, performances with the Zephyr Trio, and visits to the house of a beautiful young woman named Myrtle Ellis, a fine pianist on whom I had a terrific crush. Not to mention my day job in the piano shop and an extra job, for eight and sixpence a week, delivering newspapers.

My life had already changed dramatically through the efforts of Douglas and Muriel Dawn, and I was about to take an even bigger leap.

The Dawns continued their generous habit of taking me with them to concerts. There was one evening I was especially looking forward to: a performance by the Wigmore Ensemble, with Muriel's former teacher, Geoffrey Gilbert.

Gilbert was my favorite flutist—I listened to him on the BBC's Third Programme every chance I got. But hearing him live was simply amazing. The Wigmore Ensemble played the Debussy Trio for Flute, Viola, and Harp and Beethoven's Serenade in D for Flute, Violin, and Viola. All the players were excellent, but Gilbert was something else. I was especially struck by how beautifully and softly he played the high notes—which, as I've mentioned, is one of the harder things to do on the flute. The entire evening was simply exalting.

On top of that, Gilbert and Muriel had stayed in touch, and she had told him about me. She and Douglas took me backstage to meet him after the concert, and I asked whether I might see his flute up close. He showed it to me, a very special instrument by the French flute maker Louis Lot. I was already in seventh heaven, and then Gilbert said that he would be glad to hear me play the next day.

Of course, there had to be a snag to keep this from going too smoothly. When I told the foreman in the piano shop that I had to go out for a bit to play for a famous visiting flutist, he took on as if he wasn't going to let me go. Finally he did, but grudgingly. "All right, young fellow," he said, "but hurry up and get it over and get back here quickly." He wouldn't even let me take off the filthy green coverall that I wore while sanding piano keys and cleaning glue pots. I was humiliated, but nonetheless I hurried down the street to a studio Muriel had rented for the occasion.

Gilbert began by asking, politely but firmly, "Why are you late?" I stammered something—I didn't want to tell him what kind of man I worked for—and I was so embarrassed, I don't remember exactly how we got off that topic. But in any case, I started doing what I had come to do and played a Mozart concerto.

When I had finished, Gilbert turned not to me but to Muriel. He asked her, "How did you teach that lad to phrase like that?"

She told him, "I didn't. He's phrasing differently today because he heard you play last night. He always picks up the best out of everything he hears."

Gilbert said, "I've never come across anything like it. I want to teach him."

The two of them went back and forth over how this might be managed, because I could scarcely afford a trip to London to audition at the Guildhall School of Music, where Gilbert taught. But he said not to worry—the Guildhall would accept me on his say-so. And Muriel said, "I promise you, I won't let anybody else have him. He will go to you."

But this still didn't solve the problem of where I would get the money to go to London, let alone pay for my tuition. Here again, Douglas came to the rescue. As musical adviser to the Belfast Education Committee, he had been trying for some while to persuade the committee to give grants to underprivileged children. The committee had finally agreed, and so, along with several other kids, I turned up at an old building on Academy Street to audition for a grant. There were several of my friends there, and I think we all got grants. Mine was specifically for me to go and study in London for three years.

But there was yet another problem: my parents were frantic at the thought of my living in London. I was only fifteen, with no experience of life at all. I was streetwise enough on my own turf, from tooling around town with my mates. But except for one family trip to Dublin and a few holidays in Bangor, a seaside town just a few miles away, I had never been out of Belfast. Douglas suggested that I could stay with some friends of his, but Muriel was adamant that this wouldn't do, for reasons she didn't explain. In those days, the Guildhall didn't offer any sort of housing for its students.

While all of this was going on, John Francis showed up in Belfast. He was another high-level flute player and friend of Muriel's. He had come to Belfast to give a recital with his wife, the pianist and harpsichordist Millicent Silver. He had a gold-plated Louis Lot, and that made a huge impression on me.

Muriel suggested that he might want to hear me play, so he came to her house for my lesson the following day. I left when I finished playing, but Muriel told me what happened next. John Francis also wanted to teach me—he taught at the Royal College of Music in London. Muriel was firm: "He's going to Geoffrey Gilbert for lessons—and he's not going to anybody else."

Francis seemed to accept that, but then the next day he turned up on the Dawns' doorstep. "Look, I haven't been able to sleep all night thinking of that boy. I want to teach him."

As I said, Geoffrey Gilbert was so angry with Muriel Dawn when she recommended that I study with John Francis that he broke off their friendship. But he did make it up with her, and they were both there when I received my doctorate from the University of Ireland. Geoffrey and Muriel are on my right; my good friend Irene Burri is on my left.

Muriel repeated that I was going to Geoffrey Gilbert, but Francis played his trump card: "When he comes to London, who's going to look after him? Is he capable of looking after himself at his age? If you let him come to me, I'll take him into my house and treat him as one of the family." Francis paused for a moment and then said, "I wish I were a great enough person to say I'll take him into my house and let him go to anybody else he wants for lessons—but I can't. If I take him in, I'll want to teach him."

This put Muriel in a terrible position, but she felt that she had to tell my father about this offer. My dad went back and forth on it a bit, but he finally said, "It's in your hands, missus—you decide." Then Muriel and Douglas talked it over, and she finally decided she had no choice. She wrote to Geoffrey Gilbert to break the news, and he was so angry, he broke off their friendship—although he finally made up with her several years later.

Of course, I was terribly disappointed, too—I admired John Francis, but Geoffrey Gilbert was my hero. Yet I knew I wasn't capable of living on my own, and I did want to study in London. We made the arrangements with John Francis, and I prepared to leave for England.

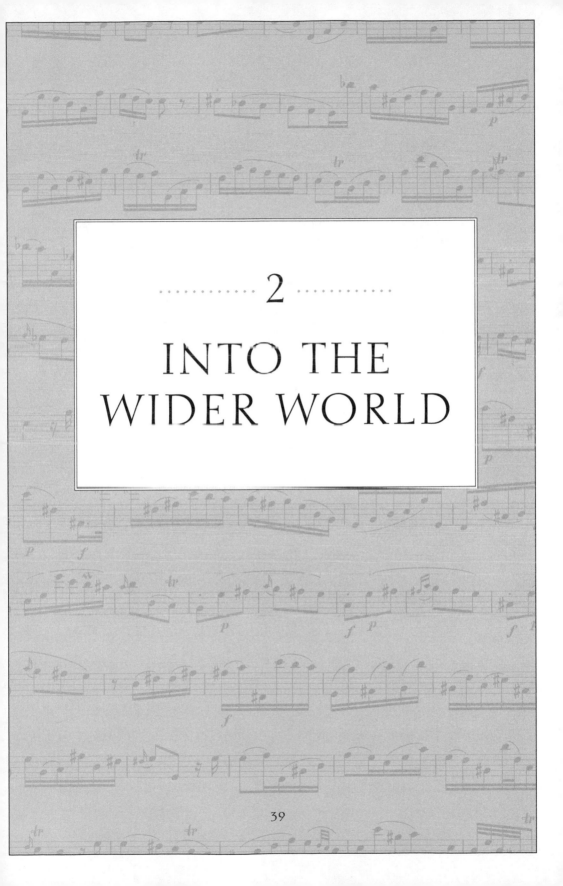

2

INTO THE
WIDER WORLD

GOING TO LONDON WAS A REAL ADVENTURE FOR the fifteen-year-old me. In retrospect, it seems amazing that my parents would let me do this unaccompanied, but I suppose they thought nothing much could go wrong on the voyage, and in fact nothing did. I had my little suitcase with my flute in it and what few clothes I owned, and I boarded the ferryboat right in Belfast for the trip to Heysham. That was a really rough ride, as it often is. I stopped taking the ferry a long time age, once I could afford to fly, but, of course, flying was out of the question for me in those days.

At Heysham I managed to find the right train, and in just a few hours we arrived at Euston Station, London. John Francis had come to meet me, and when he led me to his car, it turned out to be a Rolls-Royce. I could hardly believe that. Back home, only one guy in the entire neighborhood had a car, and it was just a little Austin 7. He was named Geordie Robinson, and he lived one street over from Carnalea Street. Geordie was in the B Specials (aka the Ulster

Special Constabulary), and he always came charging by with a bunch of guns in his car on the way to work. I remember the registration number to this day, 0Z9. Sometimes he passed by with a rifle in the back of his car, and this earned him the nickname "Sheriff." He had a lot of power over the kids in the neighborhood. I remember very well one time when we were burning an old tire that we'd found, just for the fun of it, and he threatened to shoot us if we did not put out the fire. His racing pigeons were flying through the thick black smoke, and I guess his prize birds must have come home a little darker than when they'd left his loft.

John and Millicent had a big house with a magnificent garden on Marlborough Place in St. John's Wood, just around the corner from where the famous photograph was taken of the Beatles striding across Abbey Road on the black and white stripes of the crosswalk. Quite a few prominent people lived in this neighborhood. Directly opposite John and Millicent was the composer Sir Arthur Bliss, who had just been named Master of the Queen's Music (or "Musick," as he insisted on spelling it, after the fashion of Charles I). Also nearby was the controversial barrister (and later judge) Christmas Humphreys. And around the corner was the civil servant and diplomat Sir John Maud (later Lord Maud) and his wife, Jean. They went to the same church that I did, St. Mark's in Hamilton Terrace, and from time to time they invited me to their house for tea.

Now, John and Millicent didn't go to church themselves, but they made sure that I went. Not that they had to push me. I was eager to get instruction in the Bible and in the ways of Christ, and I wanted to be part of a church, part of a group of like-minded people. Later in my life, I fell off the wagon there for a couple of years, but I got back on it—thank God.

The Francises' house had music coming out of every room all day long. John and Millicent had a group called the London Harpsichord Ensemble, which was very much in demand in London and all around the United Kingdom, so they practiced whenever they weren't teaching. I learned that Millicent had an important place in English keyboard history: the harpsichord had fallen out of favor somewhere along the line, and Millicent was one of a handful of people who revived it at the end of World War II.

Of course, both of their daughters were also musicians—Sarah played the oboe; Hannah sang and played the harp. They have gone on to fine professional careers, and Sarah took over the London Harpsichord Ensemble when Millicent and John retired in the early eighties.

Other students besides me lived and practiced in the Franciscs' house. I remember a pianist named Diana Koshiden, whose father, I was told, was lord chief justice of Ghana, and a violinist named David Roth, who went on to have a fine career, notably with the Allegri String Quartet. It was through listening to David and his friends that I became familiar with the fine repertoire of the string quartet, and a love of this repertoire is still with me. I'll never forget the Beethoven quartets as I first heard them played by David and his friends across the hall from my room.

John was true to his word about treating me as one of the family. Whenever he and Millicent took Sarah and Hannah on a holiday anywhere, they took me, too. Millicent really became a second mother to me. When I needed clothes or shoes, she and John used a little of my grant money to pay for them, but nothing like the full cost. If I wanted an extra lesson, John let me pay for it by helping Millicent with her shopping or by washing his Rolls. (The latter actually wasn't my favorite chore, because the Rolls was as big as a house.) John and Millicent also continued the good work that Douglas and Muriel Dawn had begun, broadening my horizons in all sorts of ways. John took me to hear the Royal Philharmonic for one of Sir Thomas Beecham's last concerts—it was in the BBC's Maida Vale studios, and the program included the *Jupiter* Symphony—and to Covent Garden for my first ballet, *The Prince of the Pagodas*, set to music by Benjamin Britten. He and Millicent also took me to the National Gallery and the Tate and introduced me to the paintings of Turner and Blake. The Blakes really knocked me sideways—I had

In the mid-1950s, when I was fifteen or so, with Etta Goult on the piano.

never seen anything like them. I even started to read some of Blake's poetry.

One of John's eccentricities was his preferred way of getting about London. If it was just himself, or him and me, instead of revving up the Rolls, he wheeled out his old gray motorbike. John had been a policeman during the war and had used this bike for doing the rounds. It didn't matter how cold it was—off we went, half freezing, me bare-headed, while he wore a great Russian fur hat. I was mostly scared to death, because John was not a remarkable driver, to say the least.

Yet all of this, exciting as it was, was secondary to my real reason for being in London: to learn to play the flute as well as I possibly could. I still yearned to go and study with Geoffrey Gilbert, but I had to admit that John was a fine teacher. I also learned a fair amount at the Royal College itself, although I found the curriculum much heavier on music history and theory than suited me. One teacher I remember with great admiration was Harry Stubbs. He taught me harmony, but he did much more than that: he helped me to get *inside* the music, to feel it as a living thing. Another was Ernest Hall, a famous London trumpet player who coached the wind sections of both of the college's orchestras. (When I started at the Royal College, I entered the second orchestra; the following term, I was promoted to the first one.) Hall had played with most of the best orchestras in England, and his knowledge of music was wide and deep. If you asked him how something should sound, he could draw on his vast experience to help you play it better. Another of my favorite teachers was a bassoonist named Archie Camden, who finally solved a problem that had plagued me from my earliest days on the flute: playing accurately in 6/8 time. One day when I was royally messing up the flute part in Beethoven's Seventh, Archie stopped the class and turned to me. "Listen," he said, "this rhythm is really very easy. All you've got to do is think, 'Amsterdam, Amsterdam, Amsterdam.'" He was right: it worked. In fact, from that day on, whenever I played Beethoven's Seventh in orchestras, I would mentally sing, "Amsterdam, Amsterdam, Amsterdam," to keep myself in line.

Muriel had started me out on Marcel Moyse's famous book on tone production, *De la Sonorité*. One day during a lesson, John played for me a recording by Moyse of the famous flute solo by Doppler called "Fantaisie Pastorale Hongroise," and it took my breath away. I listened to it several times a day for well over a year, and I would say that it, more than anything else I ever heard, had the biggest influence on me and the way I wanted to play the flute. I had thought Geoffrey Gilbert was great, and he was. But this was flute playing quite simply at another level.

I immediately tried to copy Moyse, although this led to some friction with John. I didn't understand why at the time, but eventually I realized that John believed in playing the music precisely in time, as if there were a metronome going—click, click, click, click, click. Now, I don't know how to express myself that way. Imagine if you were in a Shakespeare play, and all the words had to come out mechanically to a certain tempo, instead of varying as a mark of expression and feeling and deep thought. So John and I occasionally disagreed.

Many years later, when I had met Moyse and we had become friends, I asked him, "Did you ever try to play the flute like Philippe Gaubert?"—that was his teacher, who was a wonderful flute player. And Moyse said, "Oh, yes, every day of my life. But then one day I thought, Well, it's not so bad to be Marcel Moyse." And I had come to a similar realization after a long period of trying to imitate Moyse—I thought, It's not so bad playing the flute like James Galway.

In any case, John's absolute favorite composer, and Millicent's, was Bach. They had Bach's complete works in their amazing library, and likely as not, an assignment from John would be Bach. We wrangled a bit over his trying to make me learn the B Minor Sonata, a huge piece of music that I couldn't get my mind around. I would rather have played nineteenth-century virtuoso works, such as those by Paganini. But eventually I got the hang of it and came to love Bach, even if not quite to the extent that John and Millicent did.

At the end of the school term, I went home to Belfast for the summer. I was able to visit my family and friends that way, but truthfully, in terms of what I did with myself most of the time, I might as well have stayed in St. John's Wood. I had brought the Moyse studies with me, and I played them to death, hour after hour, day after day. In one sense, it wasn't a holiday at all, but it made a tremendous difference in my playing, and I considered it time well spent.

Back in London, my best friend, apart from the Francises, was another flute player named William Bennett. Wibb, as he is affectionately known, went on to a great career and also helped influence the design of modern flutes. He was three years older than I, tall and handsome and a bit of a prankster, always coming up with practical jokes. He was ahead of me on various flute techniques, and he was also where I wanted to be, studying with Geoffrey Gilbert at the Guildhall.

I often turned to Wibb for technical advice, just as I had learned from other fellows in the flute bands as a kid, and he was always glad to help me out. For example, I had trouble linking one note to a higher note in legato passages. Wibb gave me some Moyse exercises that I hadn't run across before, and he also showed me some fingerings that were different from the academically "correct" ones that I had been taught. Gradually, as these fingerings became second nature to me, they solved my legato problem.

Another problem I had was that my playing had a softness I didn't like. I don't mean soft as opposed to loud; I mean that I sort of slid into a note instead of getting the "Ping!" that my favorite flutists had—players like Moyse and Gilbert. As it happened, when I first mentioned this, Wibb had recently been to Paris, and he had learned the trick. "I know now how to do this," he told me, "to *attack* a note on the flute." The technique was called *détaché*, he told me, and it proved not to be difficult once you knew the trick, which was to put your tongue much farther forward than I had been doing. As with the fingerings, though, it takes a lot of practice to get it into your muscles. I kept working away, practicing the *détaché* all the way up and down the flute until I finally had it. It's especially difficult on the low notes.

Wibb often took me to visit his family. His father, Frank Bennett, was a successful architect who didn't think much of his son's chosen field. "Tell me, James," he said to me one Sunday at the lunch table, "do you really think you will ever make a living just blowing a flute? I sometimes wonder about William." (Frank Bennett did live to see Wibb and me become full-fledged professionals, though I don't believe he was still around when Wibb started to make a name for himself with the English Chamber Orchestra, or when I became first flute with Europe's most prestigious orchestra, the Berlin Philharmonic.)

Of course, only a year or two earlier in Belfast, it had never occurred to me, either, that I could play the flute as a full-time professional. An occasional paying gig was the most I aspired to. But studying in London had changed that. I even had the temerity to look beyond joining the flute section of an orchestra and dream of being a soloist. Now, when I spoke of these dreams out loud, my fellow students were quick to let me know I was daft. "There's nothing to play on the flute!" they said. "You'll never make it." The violin and the piano were different—even the cello. The best soloists on those instruments were international stars. But who besides Jean-Pierre Rampal had ever made it to that level on the flute?

I had a sneaking feeling that they were right, yet I still went ahead and studied the solo flute repertoire. And John Francis was wonderful about encouraging me, digging into his fabulous music library for pieces I should learn. This later served me well when I came to audition for orchestras, especially in my famous audition for the Berlin Philharmonic, which I'll describe in due time.

Meanwhile, if I was to earn a living once I finished school, I would have to get into an orchestra, and the only way to learn to play in an orchestra is to do it. So, besides the college orchestra,

I joined the London Junior Orchestra. Like my fellow students, I also took whatever gigs I could get with other orchestras and groups. Many of these we did without pay, for the experience, but some of them did pay a bit. Not that I needed a lot of money, thanks to John and Millicent. So I saved up whatever I made, which meant that when I came across a beautiful Haynes flute in the shop of Bill Lewington, I was able to purchase it. I played this Haynes for years, until I bought my first Cooper flute. Even then I kept the Haynes headpiece and used it on the flutes Mr. Cooper made for me, right up through the Berlin Philharmonic audition and my first two years in the orchestra.

Much as I loved living with the Francises, I hadn't lost my yearning to study with Geoffrey Gilbert. In fact, my friendship with William Bennett had probably increased it. So one day I picked up the phone and rang Gilbert and asked whether he would possibly give me lessons on the side.

Although I knew that he had wanted to teach me as much as I wanted to be taught by him, he refused. "I'm sorry, Galway," he said, "but it would be completely unethical for me to teach you, or even give you lessons, while you are under tuition with John Francis."

"Is there no way, then?" I replied.

"Only by resigning from the Royal College and leaving your present teacher, I'm afraid."

And so, painful as it was to break the news to John and Millicent, who had been kinder to me than I can say, that's what I did. After three years with them, I left their beautiful house and went home to Belfast, where Douglas Dawn helped me get my scholarship grant transferred from the Royal College to the Guildhall.

When I returned to London, the first thing I needed to do was find a place to live. A friend of mine, Robert Dawes, who played the flute with the BBC Concert Orchestra, was also looking for a flat, and we teamed up and found one in Notting Hill—about as far removed from St. John's Wood in socioeconomic terms as you could get in those days, although Notting Hill has since come up in the world. The flat we found was on the top floor of a house in Lansdowne Road. It was fairly grim. It came furnished, but the furniture was nothing to write home about. In the small kitchen, Bob installed a lathe, on which he made bits and pieces for his car, a little Messerschmitt KR200. Whenever the engine needed repairs, we carried it upstairs. We had to do this when the landlady was out, as she did not take kindly to our turning the top floor of her house into a working garage.

When I was offered a job for the summer, playing show tunes with an orchestra in the Pavilion in Bexhill, I was only too happy to take it. We said good-bye to our landlady, and we both moved out. I found a flat in South London, and Bob went off and got married to his girlfriend, Dori Firth.

Bexhill is a seaside resort in Sussex, about fifty miles south of London—too far to travel every day. So I hunted around for lodgings and had the great good luck to knock on the door of a Mr. and Mrs. Carter, who were kindness itself. Many years later, when I had made my first solo recording, Mrs. Carter wrote to me, "Jimmy, if I'd known you were going to do something like this when you were living in my house, I wouldn't have complained so much when you were practicing your scales." I don't actually remember her complaining that much, though; what I remember is how she took me in and made me one of the family.

My luck held when I returned to London in the fall and found another wonderful landlady, Jo Dodd. She lived just south of the Thames on Borough High Street, which runs straight across London Bridge. Her house, no. 211, had been the jailer's home at Marshalsea Prison, the debtors' prison where Charles Dickens's father was locked up and where Dickens set *Little Dorrit*. In fact, when you looked out a window at the back of Jo's house, you saw the prison. Of course, it had since been converted into some sort of factory.

Dashing and sophisticated at age seventeen, at Bexhill-on-Sea, in 1957.

Through no fault of Jo's, I quickly turned my attic room into a pigsty, but she treated me and my fellow lodgers well, and she had a great advantage when it came to my practicing scales: being almost stone-deaf, all that she had to do was turn off her hearing aid.

Apart from my playing with a wonderful bunch of people in the Bexhill orchestra, what had made that summer memorable was Annabelle. I'd had plenty of infatuations before, but I thought that what I had with Annabelle Lancaster was the real thing. I had met her when I came back from Belfast through some girls I knew at the Royal College, and we spent every moment we could together. When I was in Bexhill, I called her every day, and I came back to London every weekend to be with her. But somehow she drifted away from me, and for a while I was inconsolable. For the first time since I'd started playing the flute, I didn't even want to practice. Life goes on, though, and once I started to study with Geoffrey Gilbert, I pulled out of my despondency.

Not that my first lesson was very auspicious. I went to his house on Maida Vale, just a couple of blocks away from where the Francises lived. The Gilberts' house was as beautiful as the Francises' and not as hectic, because there weren't music students playing or singing in every corner. When you went into the music room, the first thing that struck you, apart from the grand piano, was a hanging on the wall. It was a Chinese, or maybe Japanese, tapestry of a bird, and it was a lovely thing.

Instead of bringing in an accompanist, Geoffrey Gilbert sat down at the piano himself, and he played beautifully—which is not that common among masters of another instrument. I played two sonatas, the Prokofiev and the Hindemith, and felt pretty pleased with myself. But the first thing he said was, "Tell me, Galway, do you play everything as loud as that?" I was quite miffed—among other things, William Bennett, who was also Geoffrey's pupil, played at least as loud as I had. And I replied, "Only when the piano is loud." Talk about putting your foot in it!

Geoffrey gave me a list of things to study, and I worked hard to be able to play them as well as I possibly could in my next lesson. When I arrived at his house the following week, he asked whether I had practiced my scales. I said yes. I asked him which one he wanted to hear, and he calmly said, "All of them." Well, I nearly died, but I managed to play them all. Then he asked me about my études. He had given me a book of études by the famous Italian flute virtuoso Leonardo de Lorenzo, and I began to struggle slowly through the first one. He stopped me and got his own flute out of its case. He played the study from beginning to end at a blistering speed.

These first two lessons weren't among my happiest hours, but I had indeed been right to want to study with Geoffrey Gilbert. I had benefited in so many ways from my time with John Francis, not least from his introducing me to new worlds of music and art and theater. John had given me a solid foundation of flute repertoire and had helped me bring my technique up to a certain point. But now Geoffrey built on what John had done, just as John had built on what Muriel and Douglas Dawn had done.

I had already learned from Muriel, for example, the importance of being able to play evenly all the way up and down the flute, and I had been working on that ever since. Now Geoffrey helped me finally achieve it. He had a particular scale method that worked very well for me, and he also drilled me in playing notes above the staff until I could do it consistently.

One of his great strengths as a teacher was not overwhelming the student with too many new things at once. He could diagnose just what points the student should be working on at a given time, and then when you'd done that for a week or two, he would bring in the next point, and so on, until it started to make sense at a new level. Perhaps even more important, he helped me find my own style, my own personal way of playing. I had known intuitively that the fusion, you might say, of the player with the music was what I responded to in the recordings of Marcel Moyse and in Geoffrey's own playing. Now he helped me achieve that as well.

Geoffrey also had a nice sense of humor that I appreciated. I recall one occasion that could have turned out quite differently if he had been a less even-tempered sort of man. By this time I was beginning to be noticed by the musical gentry, so to speak, and one day I got a phone call asking whether I would come up to Manchester for a gig. I was to play second flute for the BBC Northern Symphony Orchestra. As I've mentioned, I took every chance I got to play with professional orchestras, so I accepted, although I was scheduled to have a lesson with Geoffrey that same day. I called up his house, and when Mrs. Gilbert answered, I told her that I had diarrhea and needed to cancel my lesson. Many of us students used this excuse when we wanted to get out of something.

I took the train to Manchester in time for the rehearsal. I came in and sat down, waiting for the rehearsal to begin, when I noticed that the Nielsen flute concerto was on the program. Just imagine how I felt when none other than Geoffrey Gilbert walked into the rehearsal. He shook hands with the conductor and a few friends in the orchestra, and then he spied me. Looking straight at me, he said, "Oh, there you are, Galway. I thought you were ill."

"I was, as a matter of fact," I stammered.

"Well, you'd better come for your lesson tomorrow, don't you think?"

My grant to study with Geoffrey was for only one year, so when that time drew to a close, I had to decide what I would do next. I had become a pretty decent flute player by then, but there are a lot of pretty decent flute players around. The question was how to give myself an edge.

It was Geoffrey who suggested the Paris Conservatoire. After all, the French style was generally considered the best, and I clearly had an affinity for it, given my reaction to Moyse. But, of course, I would need another grant of some sort.

Fortunately, I had met and become friendly with the French cultural attaché, Tony Mayer. An attaché at an embassy is not usually a great public figure, but Tony had made quite a mark on London and the United Kingdom generally. He had come to London in 1940, responding to General de Gaulle's famous BBC broadcast calling on all French citizens who could escape the Nazi occupation to join him in fighting from England. Even during the war, Tony organized concerts of French music in London, and in 1945 he became the cultural attaché. He had ties throughout both the French and the English musical worlds.

I called on him one day at his rather grand house, which was in Eaton Square, in Belgravia, and he told me that if I wanted to apply for a grant, he would see what he could do. A few days later, he sent word that I should come to his office. When I walked in, the first thing he said was, "Look, Jimmy, do you really want to play the flute?"

This was the constant refrain I had heard at the Royal College and the Guildhall, where everyone pushed the pianists and the violinists and relegated flutists, so to speak, to second fiddle.

Now, in Tony Mayer's office, when I said, yes, I did want to play the flute, Tony countered with, "You wouldn't like to be a conductor? Or something?"

No, I explained, I didn't want to be a conductor or something. I wanted to play the flute.

He sighed and then said, "Okay, Jimmy, I'll arrange an audition for you."

He was as good as his word, and I dutifully went to my audition at the French Institute in South Kensington. When I learned that I had been accepted and had won a scholarship, I immediately turned to Tony for help in getting organized. I had been to the Continent only once before, and not on my own—I had gone to Vienna with the London Junior Orchestra, and its managers had taken care of all of the arrangements.

Now Tony helped me with travel plans and visas and everything. Even that went beyond what would be expected of him as cultural attaché, but what he did next went *way* beyond. One day when I came to see him, he said, "Jim, you'll at least need a new jacket." So he took me to a shop in the West End and bought me a beautiful jacket, far and away the nicest I had ever owned. Then he said, "You've been working hard—and you've an even harder period ahead of you." So he told me that when I arrived in France, before I got settled in Paris, I should take a holiday at his house, La Carmegan, in the Vaucluse region, near Avignon. Except for trips to the seashore when I was a kid and then to various places in England with John and Millicent and their daughters, I had never spent time outside a city, and I had certainly never been in the countryside on my own. The vacation was very exciting and different, and I felt that Tony's generosity was truly extraordinary.

The Conservatoire would prove to be something else again.

First, it had to be determined what class I would be in. The Conservatoire at that time had two flute classes, the *classe d'étrangers* and the *classe française*. The *class française* did accept foreigners, but only one per year. I was competing against fifty-six other young players for that one slot. The audition started with all fifty-seven of us playing at once, and you can imagine what kind of noise *that* made.

Then we were called up, one by one, to play our solos before a jury that included Rampal, Christian Lardé, and two or three other musicians who were only slightly less distinguished. When my turn came, I strode to the music stand and adjusted its height—as I've said, I'm not very tall. I had just opened my Mozart score and put my flute to my lips when an old man shuffled up and raised the stand to where it had been before. I began to play, and when I had a rest of several bars I lowered the stand again. At this, to my astonishment, the eminent members of the jury cracked up. Trying to ignore them, I kept playing, and the old man came over and put the stand back to full height again. At this point I just gave up and played my piece to the end and followed it with a French piece. At the end of the day, I won the place in the *classe française*. I later learned

At the Paris Conservatoire, in 1959. I'm at the top left, with glasses. What a bunch of gifted flute players they were!

that the "old man" was Gaston Crunelle, the revered teacher of the Conservatoire's flute class.

It was when the classes began that my disappointment set in. Except for maybe my father, all of my teachers and coaches, formal or informal, going back to Uncle Joe—and certainly Muriel and Duggie Dawn, John Francis, and Geoffrey Gilbert, not to mention William Bennett—had explained things to me: *why* I should try to play a passage a certain way; *how* I could get the effect I was trying for. Gaston Crunelle explained very little, although when he did say something, he made a real difference. Even Rampal didn't explain things in the way I was used to from my previous teachers, but he was such an inspiration that simply being in his presence was a rare gift.

Also, instead of the one-on-one lessons I was used to—where you play for your teacher, and he or she criticizes what you're doing or demonstrates what you should be doing—the classes at the Conservatoire were all group classes. Five or six of us sat there, and, one by one, each of us stood up and played his piece—each of us playing the same piece, and each trying to outdo the one before him. Dear old Crunelle, meanwhile, sat there reading his newspaper and smoking one Gauloise after another—although if you made a mistake or played a wrong note, he immediately brought it to your attention. All in all, I would say the standard of playing in that class under his leadership was the best I had ever encountered.

I later realized two things. First, that the competitive nature of those classes really spurred me to do my best. Here I was the *étranger* in the *classe française*, and I wanted to show them all what I could do. Second, at the Royal College and the Guildhall I had complained about the time spent on theory and history, not only because I didn't care for them, but because they took two or three hours a day away from what a young musician should really be doing, which is developing his muscles, laying down a solid technique, and learning the repertoire, including the orchestral repertoire. There were not enough hours in the day for me to take all of those classes and study the flute the way I thought it should be done. No matter the depth of your understanding of how a piece of music should sound, if you haven't trained your muscles when they're young and impression-able—for a flutist, the fingers as well as the facial muscles—you won't be able to produce the sounds you want. Well, at the Conservatoire no one dragged us away from our practicing, and I spent all day, every day, working on scales, arpeggios, articulation—all the things you need if you're to make it as a professional flutist.

Meanwhile, I had made some good friends, and one of them, a French Canadian girl named Gail Grinstead, was studying with Rampal. Gail was the only girl in the class. I asked her whether she could intercede with Rampal to give me a few private lessons, and sure enough, one day he invited me to come to his home on the avenue Mozart, in the sixteenth arrondissement. (The Conservatoire was in the center of Paris, in the ninth arrondissement.) There was a baker's shop on that street called La Flûte Enchantée.

After I played for Rampal, he asked me, "Why do you want to come here?"

"I want to play in the French style, Maestro," I replied.

"But you *already* play in the French style. Better than any Frenchman."

Well, I loved the sound of that, but I still wished he had opened his stores of knowledge to me. He never did, but instead, like John Francis and the Dawns, he took me to concerts and even to l'Opéra, where he often played. To hear Rampal play in what may be the most beautiful opera house in the world, and as his guest, no less—that made a year in Paris feel like heaven on earth.

And Paris itself was magnificent. I went into every museum and art gallery I saw, but I spent the most time in the Louvre, particularly staring at the *Mona Lisa* and Delacroix's portrait of Chopin. I soaked up the glorious stained glass of the Sainte-Chapelle, although I was more wary of Notre-Dame: Belfast Protestants don't lightly go into functioning Roman Catholic churches. Of course, there were the smells and tastes of Paris, with plenty of street vendors catering to those who didn't have too many francs in their pockets. And speaking of francs, some of my friends and I regularly went down and busked in the *métro*. We gave good quality for the coins that clattered into our bowls; I remember playing arias from *The Magic Flute*. One day a lady said to me, "You know, you should take up music professionally."

But even though I was having a lot of fun in Paris, the Conservatoire itself was increasingly getting under my skin. Finally one day I simply told Maître Crunelle I was going to leave the class.

That probably wouldn't have been taken lightly anywhere in those days—the student revolts of the late sixties were several years in the future, and young people were supposed to know their place. Certainly, this was true at the Conservatoire. The next day I was hauled up before a board that would decide what to do about me. When I said there was nothing they could do—I was fed up and I was going to leave—they were horrified. "People don't leave the Conservatoire!" one of these distinguished gentlemen said. "People don't walk out on scholarships."

But that's just what I was going to do, and I did.

You see, students at the Conservatoire were not permitted to leave Paris during the term, and I needed to go to London right away. William Bennett had become first flute in the Sadler's Wells opera orchestra, and he had called one day to tip me off that the company's second flute had just left. However, if I wanted to apply for the position, I had to get back there to audition for it.

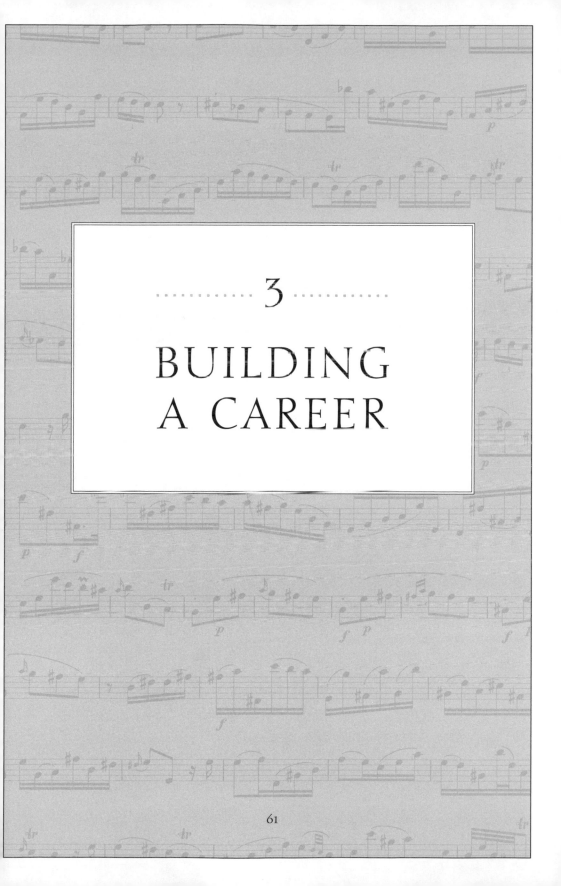

3

BUILDING A CAREER

WHEN I LEFT THE PARIS CONSERVATOIRE, I WAS done with schooling (though not, of course, with learning; that goes on as long as you're alive). I was ready to start building a professional career.

Actually, in a very real sense I had started to do that many years earlier, as a kid in Belfast. I seldom got paid for playing in those days, but every time you stand up in front of an audience, you gain experience. So all of those times I played solo or in the trio with Billy and Edmund, at nursing homes and the like, not to mention with the flute bands and the youth orchestra, I was laying a foundation of practical musical experience.

I had built on it during my time in London, when my friends and I got occasional gigs with semiprofessional orchestras and amateur opera companies. Then, during the summer between my leaving the Guildhall and going to Paris, I was hired to play in the pit orchestra at the Royal Shakespeare Theatre in Stratford-upon-Avon. Peter Hall had just taken over the company, and it was interesting to be there, to say the least. I hadn't cared for the acting students I ran into at the Guildhall; they had seemed awfully full of themselves. But the real actors at Stratford—people such as Peter O'Toole, Max Adrian, Dorothy Tutin, and Jack MacGowran—were all very pleasant and socialized with everyone, including the musicians.

My best friend in Stratford was Norman Archibald, who played the trumpet. We didn't play on the weekends in Stratford, and so Norman was able to sub with the London Symphony Orchestra. And Norman had a car. This made it easy for him to take me along to London every weekend. I'm afraid I was not the greatest company in the world, as I would fall asleep as soon as we got going. Sleeping in cars is something I do to this day—it is a very good thing that I've never learned to drive.

Every time Norman played with the LSO, he would bring me to the rehearsal, and he usually got me tickets for the evening performance. I thought that was wonderful—here I was, getting to listen to all of these great players, like Henryk Szeryng and Mstislav Rostropovich and Martha Argerich, every weekend. I really feel indebted to Norman for taking charge of my musical education at that time. Little did I know that in just nine years' time I would be solo flute in this great orchestra.

Everything I had done so far had been a tremendous experience, but it all seemed temporary. Now I had to think about the long term.

After announcing that I was leaving the Conservatoire, I quickly packed up and caught the next ferry back to England. Fortunately, my landlady, Jo Dodd, had kept my old room for me, so all I had to do in the way of housing was move back in. Then there was the matter of Sadler's Wells.

As Wibb Bennett had suggested, I rang the offices there to apply for the second-flute position. I was invited to come in and audition for Alexander Gibson, the principal conductor, and two of his colleagues: concertmaster John Ludlow and a member of the company's administration.

Gibson—"Wee Alex," as he was known—started off by asking me to do a sight reading. When you're asked to sight-read, you always hope you won't actually have to: in other words, you hope that what they choose will be something you've played somewhere along the line. I was lucky: Gibson asked for a passage from *Carmen* that I knew pretty well. Then he wanted a couple of other passages, and I was doing fine. But Alex Gibson hadn't got where he was without having a few tricks up his sleeve. He walked over to the piano and played some fifths that sounded like the drone of a bagpipe. "If I were to play this," he asked, "what would you play on top of it, Jimmy?"

I thought for a moment and then struck up an Irish jig.

Alex laughed and stood up. "Okay, Jimmy," he said, "you've got the job."

That was very exciting—not a one-time gig but a permanent position, even if it was *second* flute. There was just one hitch: I wouldn't see my first paycheck until rehearsals began in August. I had to find a job to fill the gap.

If I had ever thought I'd been bored before, I had no idea of the level of boredom that lay in store for me in a nuts-and-bolts warehouse. This warehouse was located on Union Street in the Borough, so I could walk to work. That was the only good thing about it. Yet this was the only job I could get, and I needed it. I don't know which I enjoyed more: the intellectual challenge of counting out seven hundred very small nuts and bolts and putting them in a box for shipping, or the helpful attitude of the coworker who had been told to teach me my job. On the first day, he showed me what to do and then went off for a while. I finished what he had assigned me and sat down to read the *Times*.

Half an hour later, he returned and asked how I was doing.

"Oh, I finished the lot," I replied.

"What?" he yelled. "Listen, Galway, never do that again! Slow it down, man, that's an order! Otherwise, the bosses will have you at it all day."

The only change of pace came when the elevator operator—in the idiom of the time, he was known as the "lift boy," though he was actually a grown man and nearly seven feet tall—went on holiday, and I was told to fill in for him. I soon figured out that once I had ferried people upstairs in the morning, I could take the lift to the top floor, go out on the roof, and enjoy the fresh air for an hour or so before I had to make a run down to see what or who needed to be moved about. This lasted for two weeks. Then the regular lift boy came back, and I was returned to counting nuts and bolts—and also counting the days until I could quit and go back to music.

One morning when I arrived for work, there was a great commotion. The company had a huge safe in the stairway, on the landing to the second floor, and during the night, someone had blown the door right off the safe and cleaned out all the contents. Well, the police came around and started questioning us all. When it was my turn to be investigated, they all burst out in laughter when I opened my mouth and replied in a very broad Belfast accent, assuring them that I did not do it and that I didn't know who did. Luckily, they believed me. And, between us, I *didn't* do it.

Finally, the happy day arrived when I could leave the nuts and bolts behind. I found myself at Sadler's Wells meeting my new mates—I remember especially Tom Kelly on clarinet, Tony Randall on horn, and on oboe Philip Jones, who became a lifelong friend. We had already started rehearsals for the new season when we got what seemed like bad news for us: Alex Gibson, who was a terrific musician, was moving on to become principal conductor and artistic director of the Royal Scottish National Orchestra. He was the first native-born Scot to hold that position. Within three years, he would found Scotland's first permanent opera company.

The big question for us, of course, was who would succeed Alex, and that proved to be very good news indeed: it was Colin Davis, only thirty-two years old, and just beginning to be spoken of as one of the great conductors. He had made the musical world sit up and take notice when he stood in for an ailing Otto Klemperer and conducted a magnificent *Don Giovanni* at the Royal Festival Hall.

The whole company responded to Colin's arrival with great enthusiasm. There was a buzz of excitement in the orchestra pit and among the singers onstage. Colin's stick technique was so clear, he was a joy to play for, and he was full of energy. His way of speaking to the orchestra was also very different from anything we had encountered before. One day during a rehearsal, he paused and said to the orchestra, "Why don't you play this phrase with truth and meaning?" We realized that this was no run-of-the-mill conductor. The orchestra soon began to sound better, and his energy started to rub off on us.

He addressed the question of personal appearance just as directly Members of the orchestra and chorus would often turn up unshaven and carelessly dressed. They looked sloppy and untidy. Colin, in his straightforward manner, said, "Now, look here. It's time, I think, we stopped being so lax about things. I think it's time everybody made up their minds to present themselves at their best."

That approach easily could have backfired, except that by then, we had experienced Colin's intense musicality and his desire to make the orchestra a crucial part of the opera, instead of simply a prop to allow the singers to perform up there on the stage. He fired us up and made us want to help him achieve his conception of the music.

We did a lot of Mozart with Colin—that was his specialty in the opera. I remember that we did *The Marriage of Figaro* with him and also *Idomeneo*. The leading role in *Idomeneo* is very difficult, but we had a wonderful tenor, Ronald Dowd, to sing it. *Idomeneo* was a raging success, and the house was sold out every night. We also did *Carmen*, and that was great too. But the highlight of Colin's career there, for me, was *The Flying Dutchman*. I had never played a Wagner opera before, and in fact I had fallen asleep when I was taken to see *Rheingold*, while I was traveling with the London Junior Orchestra several years earlier. But in Colin's hands, *The Flying Dutchman* really came to life. I loved it. A bonus was that Colin brought Stuart Knussen in on double bass to augment the orchestra. Stuart was the solo bass player of the London Symphony, and I got to meet him and came to know him fairly well afterward.

So here I was, just turned twenty and in the middle of music at a level that I had never experienced.

Not that playing with Sadler's Wells was all joy and rapture. There was the question of money, for one thing, and, more important, management's attitude toward paying us. My regular salary starting out was £21 a week (about the equivalent of $800 today)—not princely, but we knew that Sadler's Wells wasn't the richest company in the world, and you could get by. When we went on tour, we got an additional £7 a week, out of which we had to pay for our own lodging—again, not a huge sum, but you could find bed-and-breakfast places in most cities that charged £1 a night. What got under our skin was the way management handled our schedules to avoid paying us any extra. After so many "calls" a week, whether for rehearsal or performance, we were supposed to get overtime. But somehow the powers that be arranged the schedule so that we never got those extra calls.

Even so, I was able to get together the money to buy a flute from Albert Cooper, who was just becoming a very famous flute maker in London. I'll have more to say about Mr. Cooper later on, but when I turned up with this flute, everybody in the orchestra said, "Wow! Where did you get the money to buy this?" It had cost me £129—more than six weeks' salary.

"Well, you know," I said, "I don't drive, so I don't have to make the monthly payments on a car. I take the bus and the Underground."

Of course, that was easy for me because I could get a train right from the corner by Jo Dodd's house and take it to the Angel stop in Islington, right by Sadler's Wells. I used the Underground all the time.

Meanwhile, our other problem with the Sadler's Wells management was that they made it nearly impossible for us to get outside gigs, as soloists or as part of a chamber group. This mattered a lot to many of us, and not only for the money. When you're playing as part of an orchestra, it's not your own musical understanding that you're expressing, it's the conductor's. Now, with Colin, that was marvelous—yet I wanted something more.

I should explain that playing chamber music is completely different from playing in an orchestra. In chamber music, there isn't a conductor's vision being imposed on you—instead, it's three or four (or five or eight) musicians getting together and somehow working it out among themselves, so that it's as if they're all speaking with one voice. And some magnificent chamber music has been composed for the flute—Mozart and Schubert come first to mind, and Bach.

But Sadler's Wells made it very hard for us to get away to do this kind of thing. One rule was made by Colin himself, not by the front office. In retrospect, I have to admit that he was probably right, although it peeved me considerably at the time. This was his putting an end to the "deputy" system. The way it had worked was that if a player who was scheduled for a particular performance wanted to do something else, all he had to do was arrange for another player to cover for him. This had always worked perfectly well, I was told. But then one night, during Colin's first year with Sadler's Wells, we were playing *La Bohème* under a guest conductor. This conductor had told us in rehearsals that he liked to use "two bars in"—meaning that he would conduct two measures to give us the tempo before we were supposed to start playing. Unfortunately, the tuba player for that evening had sent a deputy and hadn't passed along the word about "two bars in." The conductor gave his first downbeat, and the

Always, always practicing. This was probably taken in the mid-1960s.

deputy tuba player launched in. The stagehands took that as their cue to raise the curtain, and there were several minutes of pandemonium. That's when Colin put an end to deputies.

As I say, you could make a case for that, although punishing only the player who had failed to pass along the conductor's instructions might have done the trick, while leaving the rest of us a little bit of our precious freedom. But I saw no excuse at all for what the front office did: it simply denied nearly every request for a night off. This was particularly unreasonable for the flutes, because there were three of us—Wibb on first flute, me on second, and a very experienced player named Arthur Swanson on third—and we were seldom all needed in the same piece.

In fact, this is what led to Wibb's leaving Sadler's Wells, and it was part of the reason for my own departure a couple of years later. Wibb asked for a day off, and the front office refused. "*Faust* is a very important opera for the flute," they told him.

Now Arthur, who wasn't scheduled to play that night, was a thoroughly competent player, and he knew all the operas backward and forward. He could perfectly well have taken over. Wibb knew this and probably said so. In any case, management told him that if he didn't turn up that night, he needn't come back. So he didn't.

And that's how I found myself, at age twenty-one, as first flute of the Sadler's Wells Opera. This was all a bit overwhelming. It had happened so suddenly, and I sometimes found myself thinking that I didn't really belong there—a little working-class kid from Carnalea Street among all these solidly middle-class people. It wasn't that I didn't think I was good enough in terms of technique or musicianship; it was the social thing that I couldn't always shake. Also, a black mood sometimes came over me, for reasons I didn't understand. Of course, I was still young enough to think that I was the only one who had ever felt that way.

I must say, Colin was a genius at coming up with offbeat ways to pull me out of it. One day I was standing in the queue at the canteen at lunch break. Colin came over to me and said, "What's the matter, Jimmy? You look really down today."

"Yes, I am," I replied. "But I don't know why."

"All right," said Colin. "Why don't you have a good scream or something and get it all out of your system?"

I just stared at him. "What do you mean, 'have a good scream'? It's not as simple as that, you know."

"Just shout and bawl at me—*right now!*" he retorted.

So I did—I stood there in the middle of the canteen shouting abuse at my boss at the top of my lungs, while he doubled over with laughter. It was the strangest thing I'd ever experienced. But do you know what was even more amazing? It worked. It snapped me right out of it.

Another time I heard a knock at the door of my room, and Colin was standing there. "What are you doing, Jimmy?" he asked.

"Nothing," I said—truthfully enough.

"Right," he said. "Come along, then, and have a curry." We did, and again I felt much better.

Once in a while, though, I went a bit too far. I remember one concert we played in Glasgow. The way the orchestra was arranged, I was right in front of Colin, and once when he glanced down at me, I crossed my eyes at him. The next time he brought his baton down, he reached forward with it and sharply rapped my knuckles.

We did a lot of touring at Sadler's Wells, and that could get a bit wearing. But one thing that helped was that I was back together with my friend Norman Archibald, who had taken me under his wing while we were both at Stratford-upon-Avon. Now he was first trumpet at Sadler's Wells.

When we were on tour, we always got digs together, because Norman was a much more experienced guy than I was, and he looked after me. Norman was a really dedicated player, and we both practiced diligently during our off-hours. Sometimes we played pieces like the Debussy trio or a Telemann duet, just for our own enjoyment. Now, if you play the trumpet, a piece written for the flute is very hard on the lips. But Norman didn't mind. I have to say that I really enjoyed this, and whenever Norman played something, I thought it was great.

It's a good thing we enjoyed playing together, because during the daytime there often wasn't much else to do. Most of these towns were strange to us, and we didn't know our way around. But sometimes we found a bit of fun, like the day Norman and I were strolling through downtown Manchester, and we saw some televisions in a shop window. We got the idea of going in and saying that we wanted to rent one—this was basically to get a chance to talk to a good-looking girl who was working there. We asked her all sorts of questions about the different televisions, and she patiently answered them. Then, when we finally got down to the paperwork, Norman suddenly said, "Listen, do you have a gas model? Because this is for my granny, and she lives in the middle of nowhere." At first the girl looked as if she was ready to throw us out, but then she saw the humor of it and laughed as much as we did.

Sadler's Wells had some marvelous singers—Ronald Dowd, Peter Glossop, June Bronhill, William McAlpine, and David Ward, to mention just a few. Sadly, not many of them are remembered outside Britain today. One reason is that they were less likely to get recording contracts and be hired by houses like the Met or La Scala, because Sadler's Wells insisted on doing all of its operas in English. Covent Garden had started out after World War II with a mandate to do the same thing, but it wanted to attract international stars, and few of them were willing to relearn an Italian or French or German opera in English. So gradually, during the fifties, Covent Garden had started using the original languages, and when Georg Solti took over as music director in 1961, he made that his official policy.

In any case, the grass is always greener, and after four years at Sadler's Wells, I decided to try my luck at Covent Garden. I expected more money and hoped for more freedom. I did get more money (I was paid about £36 a week), and the quality of the singers at Covent Garden, not to mention the sheer scale of things, was amazing. When they did *Aïda*, you'd swear half of London was up there onstage as the Egyptian army. Also, although the queen had not yet officially made the company the Royal Opera, the theater was the Royal Opera House, and so there was the thrill of seeing the queen's insignia on the curtain every night.

As at Sadler's Wells, though, there were problems with management. Morris Smith, the orchestra manager at Covent Garden, was not ready for my freedom of spirit, and he really annoyed me. He refused to let me play gigs away from the opera, and he routinely put me on second flute, although I had been hired as first. The big difference between the two positions is that if there are any solo bits—even for a few bars—before the rest of the orchestra comes crashing in, it's the first flute who gets them, while the second flute plays along with the ensemble. Finally one day I wouldn't take it any longer. I went to Smith and said, "Look here, my contract is to play first flute. I'm not going to spend all my time playing second."

He stared at me for a minute and then said, "If you don't like it, you can leave."

I said, "Okay, I will." And I did.

Luck was with me, because Colin was still at Sadler's Wells, and in fact he was just re-forming the wind section, with Derek Wickens on oboe, Alan Hammond on bassoon, and Roy Jowitt on clarinet. These men were all fine musicians who went on to major careers (Derek and Alan at the Royal Philharmonic, and Roy at the London Symphony). Best of all, I liked them, and we saw eye to eye musically. Colin offered me my old job back, and I took it. At the end of the season, I signed a new contract with Sadler's Wells for the same money I had been making at Covent Garden.

We had fun at Sadler's Wells. During the course of an opera, there can be long periods when a particular instrument is silent, and certain diversions can help you keep up your interest. I had a little game I played with Derek. I would say, "Okay, let's close the music and see how far we can get through this opera without opening it." With another friend, a Hungarian violinist named Joseph Turban, I played chess on a little board we set up between us.

I'll never forget my first big recording session. It was with our assistant conductor, the Italian Canadian Mario Bernardi, whose *Traviata* impressed us all tremendously. (Mario later went on to become the principal conductor of the Canadian Broadcasting Corporation's Radio Orchestra.) The opera we were recording with him was *Hansel and Gretel*, and the sessions were at the EMI studio on Abbey Road, around the corner from the Francises' house. Besides the Beatles, international artists such as Maria Callas, Yehudi Menuhin, and many other fine instrumentalists and singers had made recordings there. Just walking into that studio gave me goose bumps. You were surrounded by history.

All in all, I enjoyed that period quite a lot. The only problem was that I was still sitting in the orchestra, instead of standing up in front as a soloist.

Meanwhile, I had met my first wife. One day a man I'd become friends with during my brief time in Paris rang to say that he was in town, along with two French girls, and would I meet them for a drink? One of them was his girlfriend; the other was a small, dark girl named Claire LeBastard. She was very pretty, and we were immediately attracted to each other. She stayed in London when the others went back to France, and we went around together for a while. Inevitably, the question of marriage arose. I still wasn't making a lot of money, but her family was fairly prosperous, so we basically said, "Why not?" We went to the Kensington registry office one day and became man and wife.

By this time, Colin had left Sadler's Wells for Covent Garden. I missed him, and the management of Sadler's Wells had not become any easier to deal with. For me, the final crisis came when the City of Birmingham Symphony announced a major International Woodwind Competition, with a first prize of £1,500. I requested leave to take part in the competition, but the management representative, Charles

Coverman, was digging in his heels. Finally, I said to him, "Listen, Charlie, I'll make a deal with you. Give me the time off, and if I win the competition, I'll agree to leave the orchestra, and you can get yourself somebody who'll play night and day for you."

"What happens if you don't win?" he shot back.

"Then I'll leave anyway. Okay?" We agreed on it, then and there.

I had decided to do the concerto by Carl Nielsen and the Mozart G Major, but I didn't have any cadenzas for the Mozart. So about a week before the competition, I went to my friend Edwin Roxburgh, who had taken over as first oboe when Derek Wickens went to the Royal Philharmonic. Edwin was not only a very fine oboist but also an excellent composer. I asked him whether he would write me some cadenzas. A couple of days later, he handed me the music, and I thought it was terrific. I'm sure his cadenzas are part of the reason I came in first in the flute section. Many years later, I recorded them with Rudolf Baumgartner and the Lucerne Festival Strings.

At Birmingham, the first prize was split between me and Maurice Brogue, a very fine French oboe player. I received a check for £750. This was less than I had hoped for, but I still thought this was great; I used it to replace the roof of the house Claire and I had bought in Islington, no. 25 Aberdeen Road.

True to my word, I left the Wells, as we affectionately called it, and said a happy farewell to Charlie Coverman and Barry Collins, the leader of the orchestra.

Meanwhile, I had heard there was an opening for piccolo in the BBC Symphony Orchestra. I applied for the job and got it. Douglas Whittaker was the solo flute in the orchestra, and Brian Chadwick was the second flute. We all got on very well.

Our main conductor was Sir Malcolm Sargent, or "Flash Harry," as he was called in the business. He was good-looking and very well dressed and always wore a carnation in his lapel. Not everyone liked him; some players found him condescending and difficult. But he always treated me very well, and he was a brilliant musician.

One night we were going to be playing Beethoven's Ninth. The first thing I noticed about the orchestral material was that Sir Malcolm had gone over all the parts in red pencil just to make sure we followed Ludwig's intentions. This worked well, and the result was a solid and rousing Ninth Symphony.

Sir Malcolm could be amusing, too—and not always intentionally. Once he decided to demonstrate how he wanted me to play a particular passage by mock-playing it on his baton. I saw what he meant about the tempo and the phrasing, but it was all I could do to keep from cracking up: the great man was playing the wrong side of his imaginary flute. I wish I had had a camera at that rehearsal.

Playing in the BBC Symphony also meant playing the Proms. If you don't know about the Proms, they're a great British institution, going back more than a hundred years. The idea that Robert Newman, the manager of the Queen's Hall, and the great conductor Henry Wood had back in the 1890s was to bring in audiences who were nervous about "serious" music and create an atmosphere that was far less formal than concerts usually were—and if you think about London before World War I, I'm sure that was starchy indeed. At the Proms, unlike at a normal concert or opera, audience members can walk about during the performance and even eat and drink (and in the old days, smoke). At some point in the 1920s, the BBC took over the Proms, and by the time I joined the BBC Symphony in the sixties, audiences routinely became part of the performance—they sang along, stamped their feet, and called out to the musicians. British musicians all knew the drill. The BBC broadcast the Proms, so anyone in the United Kingdom who cared about music at all had heard them, but they sometimes took foreign players aback. Once in the seventies, when I was with the Berlin Philharmonic, we were invited to play at the Proms. The great oboist Lothar Koch played the note for the orchestra, and the Prommers sang it back to him and shouted, "Bravo, Lothar!"

A special occasion each year is Last Night at the Proms. At that performance, the second half always consists of traditional and national British songs—"Land of Hope and Glory," "Rule Britannia," "Jerusalem." I played only one Last Night under Sir Malcolm. The main work was Gustav Holst's *The Planets* (despite his name, Holst was English, and *The Planets* is widely regarded as one of the finest English symphonic works). Then in the second half, I got to play "The Sailor's Hornpipe" as part of Henry Wood's *Fantasia of British Sea Songs*. Sadly, that was truly Sargent's last night at the Proms. He had been diagnosed with pancreatic cancer earlier in the summer, and at the end of the evening he handed over his baton to his successor, Colin Davis. Sir Malcolm passed away a few weeks later, much mourned by his beloved Prommers.

Before I joined the BBC Symphony, I had tried very hard to get an audition with the London Symphony Orchestra, without a doubt the finest orchestra in Britain at that time and one of the finest in the world. When I was still at Sadler's Wells, the LSO finally called me in one day, but it was a disaster. I had planned to play part of a flute concerto and some of the orchestral repertoire—but there was no piano. "Even Sadler's Wells can afford a piano!" I complained to the jury. But there simply wasn't one, and I had to play unaccompanied. The LSO people weren't impressed, and nothing came of it.

Then one day, after I had joined the BBC Symphony, the LSO called and asked me to do a gig at the Guildhall, including Haydn's *London* Symphony. The way the program was arranged, I had a free period just after the interval, and so did a chap I knew, a trumpeter named George Reynolds. We decided to slip out to the pub around the corner. I didn't want a drink in the middle of a performance, but I went along for the camaraderie.

As we were walking back, a rather imposing gentleman stopped us. Without preamble, he asked me, "How would you like to be the first flute of the London Symphony?"

Not recognizing him, I asked, "Who are you?"

"I am Ernest Fleischmann," he announced.

I knew that Ernest Fleischmann was *the* orchestral manager in London. At this point I could hear the guys laughing at the situation I had put myself in.

"I would love to be your solo flute player, but I have just signed a three-year contract with the BBC Symphony."

Fleischmann then told me that he would talk to the BBC Symphony and get them to cancel the contract. In fact, he succeeded, and I began a few weeks later to play with the LSO, replacing Alexander Murray, a very fine flutist who had been first flute there for some twelve years.

I was elated. I was about to take a seat in a crack orchestra and begin playing with musicians known not only throughout Britain but all over the world.

Just by happenstance, I experienced a particularly sweet bit of one-upmanship over this elevation in status. One day I ran into Morris Smith, the orchestra manager of Covent Garden, on the steps of the Royal College of Music, where he was teaching the trombone. "Oh, hello, Jimmy," he said, as if there had been no bad blood between us. "So, what are you up to these days, then?"

"I've just finished with the BBC Symphony Orchestra," I replied. "It's my last day with them. I've just signed a contract with the LSO. As first flute, of course."

He laughed and shook his head in amazement.

Here I must say a bit more about my predecessor in the LSO, Alexander Murray.

I met Alex when I was a student at the Royal College. He was already first flute in the LSO, and one evening I was asked to come and play as an extra in an augmented woodwind section. They were playing Beethoven's *Pastoral* Symphony with the great Romanian conductor Sergiu Celibidache. I was doing the doubling, which is to say that when the flute part was marked fortissimo, I and others especially hired for the job would join in to get the balance correct.

Alex asked me back for later concerts, and gradually I began to play more and more with the LSO. This led to a friendship, and Alex showed me some things that have stayed with me ever since those early days.

He introduced me to the Alexander Technique, which is a conscious control of the body that reduces stress through proper alignment. Having lessons in this great technique was very useful to me in my early professional days; it helped me cope with the strain of playing in leading orchestras.

Alex also reinforced the ideas Geoffrey Gilbert had planted in me on how to hold the flute and, even more important, how to sit while playing the flute. All the things Alex taught me have stayed with me, and I am certain they have been a major reason why I have never had any muscular difficulties throughout my career. This is something I am truly grateful for. That a leading professional would share his hard-earned knowledge with a young colleague is a sign of a very gifted and special man.

Alex's wife, Joan, was a dancer in the ballet of the Royal Opera House, and she and Alex often took me to dinner after a show. I was very sad when they left the United Kingdom for the United States, but I am happy to say that at least I see them once a decade or so when I am near where they live, in Champaign, Illinois.

As a professor at the University of Illinois, Alex has done a lot of research on flute making. He developed a special flute known as the Murray flute, which has many advantages over the regular Boehm flute, though I have never got into playing it.

I often think I live a very blessed life, with all these good people in it to help me along.

Joining a top-ranked symphony orchestra was something I had wanted for years, but it was the hardest work I had ever done in my life. You can't play orchestral music at a high standard simply by learning a few notes. You have to hear how your part fits into the whole and get a sense of the tone and the sound of the thing. But nearly everything I had done since I left the Conservatoire had been from the operatic repertoire. I had never played most of these big concertos and symphonies. I had to study the orchestral repertoire like a madman. Of course, there isn't much rehearsal time, and every day it's a different program—not like the opera, where you repeat each work several times in the course of the season. Whenever I wasn't practicing, I was listening to records, which I've always found to be an enormous help. One evening Colin was our guest conductor, and he gave me a ride home. He asked, "Jimmy, how do you manage in the orchestra with all this new stuff?"

"I listen to records," I replied.

Some musicians frown on that, but Colin said, "Yes, I do that myself. It's a very quick way of learning things."

By listening to recordings, you not only get to know the basic shape of the music but also begin to understand various ways of interpreting it. Listening to music has become a part of my daily life. When I am at home in Meggen, I turn on *Swiss Classics* as soon as I get out of bed and just leave it on the whole day. Of course, I don't spend all day listening to music in the bedroom. My studio is on the opposite side of the house, and when I am doing paperwork, I listen there with my super hi-fi.

At the LSO, I worried constantly about whether I could keep up, but the hard work was also exhilarating, and certainly the results in performance were magnificent. The day-to-day dealings with my colleagues were something else again. I had never before run into such a political atmosphere among the players themselves. Between management and players, yes—at both Sadler's Wells and Covent Garden—but not on the platform. At the LSO, however, any suggestion was taken as a criticism, and the top players kept to themselves, instead of trying to help the lesser players improve.

Having said that, I have to add that one of the most generous responses I ever received from a fellow player was at the LSO, from

Back home for a summer visit with my dad, in the early 1970s.

my second flute, Richard Taylor. One time we were playing the Tchaikovsky Fifth Symphony, and everything was going along fine until we came to a passage right near the end. It has lots of scales, and it's meant to be terrifically fast—but this particular rehearsal we were taking it even faster than I expected. I found that I just couldn't keep up to the tempo. Fortunately, the music is quite loud at that point, so I was able to lean over and say, "Dick, I hadn't expected this to be so quick—I can't play it."

Not pausing an instant, he came back with, "Jimmy, leave all the *tuttis* to me—that's what I'm here for. You play all the solos—that's what *you're* here for." I can't tell you how grateful I was. Well, I did manage to play it in the evening, but I was happy to have such a great colleague. Incidentally, for all the flute players reading this, Richard plays on a Hammig flute, which he has had all his life. For non-flute players, you'll learn what this means in the next chapter.

Richard was later a participant in one of the greatest experiences of my life.

It came in the middle of a tour to the United States that was quite a mixed bag of good and bad. It was my first time traveling across the ocean, and I was very excited to finally see New York City. We played some wonderful music, and Carnegie Hall is magnificent. But there was one galling aspect to the tour: for whatever reason, the administration had decided that we needed a second principal flute. I strongly objected, but when it became clear that they were adamant, I said, "Well, then, you'd better get William Bennett, because he's the best."

They did, but then they assigned our duties in a way that drove both of us wild. Instead of having one of us play first flute one day and the other the next, they had one of us play the first half of a concert and the other the second half.

Yet one thing happened on that tour that made up for everything: I met Marcel Moyse and even had some lessons with him. He had moved to the United States in the 1940s, though he frequently paid return visits to Europe. I learned that his base of operations was the Marlboro School of Music in southern Vermont, which he had cofounded, and that he lived right up the road from Marlboro, in a town called Brattleboro. It seemed to me that southern Vermont was not very far from New York City, so when we had a couple of days off, Dick and I decided to fly up there to see Moyse.

The trip started out not too well. Because of weather, the plane couldn't land where it was supposed to, and we had a long taxi ride the rest of the way. But eventually we got to Brattleboro, which turned out to be a very pretty village, and we had no trouble finding someone to tell us where Moyse lived. We hiked up the hill until we came to a wooden door with these words written on it: "Marcel Moyse. Please come in." We did, and we found Moyse and his wife both sound asleep in front of a huge television with the sound turned up full blast.

At first, I was afraid to wake him, he looked so very old and frail. In fact, he was seventy-eight, which doesn't sound terribly ancient to me today. But his face was thin and deeply lined, and he really didn't look strong. I finally shook him gently by the shoulder, and he woke up and asked, "Where you have been?" I thought he was still half asleep, but it turned out that his English was somewhat odd, even though he had been living in the United States for nearly twenty years.

I explained who we were and why we had come, and he said, "Come back in morning and play." I worried a bit over what to play and finally settled on the Bach B Minor Sonata, which had given me such trouble in my days with John Francis. Now Moyse showed me the basic structure, how to bring out the important material in this complex piece of music. If John had given me the same explanation ten years earlier, would I have understood it? Maybe not—maybe I needed the additional experience I had acquired, most of it as a professional, surrounded by many different types of music. In any case, the advice got through to me now, and I was enthralled.

When Moyse demonstrated it for Richard and me, I heard what I can only describe as a quality of sunshine in his playing. This was something I didn't have, and on hearing it, I badly wanted it. I recalled what I had thought after studying in Paris: that English teachers tend to emphasize accuracy, whereas the French insist on beauty. There was also a personal quality to his playing, a sound as distinctive as a person's voice, and that, too, I wanted.

Moyse then began to show us how to achieve these things. We came back the next day, and I played some Schubert. He told me that what I needed to do was relate my playing to singing. He had written some exercises to help develop the "vocalization" aspect of playing, and he demonstrated these for us and gave us a copy. To this day I use those exercises, and I tell my students in master classes that they should learn how to sing—not that they have to go for a career at the Met, but they should be able to sing well enough to help them hear the melody and the tone they want before they start to play a piece. These exercises also helped me develop a more flexible embouchure, which is an important part of what critics have praised in my playing.

So I had come full circle Muriel Dawn, teaching me on Moyse's principles, had warned me when I left Belfast, "Now, whatever you do, don't let anybody change your embouchure and don't let anybody change your system." Now I was changing them—on the teaching of the master himself. What I learned in those two days in that simple little house on the hillside set me on the road to new levels of playing. I had complained at the Conservatoire that no one would explain the secrets of music to me. Now Moyse, who had himself been a student (and later a teacher) at the Conservatoire, had explained and demonstrated to my heart's content.

We had a wonderful series at Carnegie Hall, with Mstislav Rostropovich as cello soloist and Istvan Kertesz (the LSO's principal conductor) and Gennady Rozhdestvensky on the podium. It was a real marathon of cello concertos for Rostropovich. I mean, he didn't play only three or four concertos over and over in the course of the series—he played about twenty-two different concertos, sometimes three in an evening, and all from memory. This was the most amazing musical feat that I've ever heard in my life. And he didn't simply play the notes. Every note had absolute life in it. It was charming; it was virtuosic; it was manly. I just fell in love with him as a musician.

One night, though, Rostropovich was ill and couldn't perform. So we played the Mahler Fourth instead, at a moment's notice, and Rozhdestvensky conducted the whole thing from memory—that, too, was phenomenal.

When it was over, we returned to London and the mixture of great music, annoying internal politics, and brilliant conductors that characterized the LSO at that time. Kertesz himself was a splendid conductor; I was lucky enough to play for him in the LSO's recordings of the Dvořák symphonies. Rozhdestvensky was magnificent, especially in the really difficult, spectacular music that he loved. We played Bartók's *Miraculous Mandarin* with him, and Ravel's *Daphnis and Chloe*. Once, after a thoroughly glorious performance of *Daphnis and Chloe*, Rozhdestvensky came right into the orchestra and dragged me out to take a bow. Orchestral musicians often feel—and often are—underappreciated. At that moment, I would have followed Rozhdestvensky into a lions' den.

Zubin Mehta was another favorite of mine. He conducted the LSO's first performance of *The Rite of Spring*. Then the next thing we did with him was Strauss's *Heldenleben* (*A Hero's Life*). There's a tricky part in that piece for the flute. It's in the second movement, where Strauss introduces the hero's enemies, and the flute theme is very staccato, very edgy. In the first rehearsal, I interrupted at that point. "Zubin," I said, "can you make your beat a bit larger there, make your gestures a bit bigger, because I can't really see them?"

"My dear Jimmy," he replied, "I've often had a *deaf* flute player, but this is the first time I've had a *blind* one." We all broke up in fits of laughter.

Another great musician who guest-conducted us was Leonard Bernstein. An incident involving him illustrates why I left the LSO after only one season. He was rehearsing us in Sibelius's Fifth Symphony, and he wasn't getting at all what he wanted. He stopped and instructed us on how he wanted the music played, then he started in again. At nine thirty exactly, about a third of the musicians simply stopped playing and left the platform. Had this ever happened to Bernstein before? I doubt it. But that was the mentality of the LSO in those days.

Not long after that, there was a major dispute involving Ernest Fleischmann and the brilliant first horn, Barry Tuckwell, whom the players had elected to be the chairman of the orchestra. I don't remember what exactly the dispute was about, but Ernest left the LSO, and I left, too.

My old friend Derek Wickens had tipped me off about an opening at the Royal Philharmonic Orchestra. I was not so enamored of the idea of moving to the RPO—musically, it was no match for the LSO at that time—but Derek and the accountant of the orchestra, Paul Harmen, made me an offer I could not refuse. They took me to the Savoy, and during dinner we discussed a deal. There was a guaranteed minimum of £4,000 a year, the equivalent of more than $100,000 today.

Financially, this was a great move, and I accepted it. But, as I say, it was a step down musically. The RPO had had its golden age, under Sir Thomas Beecham, but by the time I joined it, there were too many mediocre players mixed in among the very good ones, and the whole orchestra was simply less solid than it should have been. Also, the principal conductor, Rudolf Kempe, was technically brilliant but a bit dry for my taste. He never seemed to want to get into the soul of the music. I mean, he was a very good conductor but not my cup of tea.

So I once again found myself dreaming of bigger things, and the biggest thing going at that time, if you were an orchestral player, was the Berlin Philharmonic under Herbert von Karajan. However, it was *so* big that I never seriously allowed myself to believe that I would get there, until a couple of chance conversations set things in motion.

The first one occurred in a car coming back from Sheffield to London. The RPO had played a one-night stand in Sheffield, and then we had spent four hours the next day rehearsing for a concert of new music. Now, I love many pieces written in recent years; I've even commissioned a few, as I'll describe in due time. But "new music," in the sense that the RPO meant it—Boulez and Stockhausen and such—didn't thrill me. I did not feel that orchestras should be playing that sort of music. For me, music has to have melody, and I have never been able to hear a melody in either Boulez or Stockhausen. Later on, I met Boulez, and he told me, "I am a modernist," and I thought, Well, that's fine, but I am a romantic.

Meanwhile, the bother of going on one-night tours didn't thrill me either. As my friend drove, I was grousing away about both of these issues when he suddenly asked, "Look, Jimmy, why don't you try for the Berlin Phil?"

As far as I was concerned, he might as well have said, "Why don't you fly to the moon?" But I did begin to think about it more seriously, and I remembered hearing that Karajan had started to look outside Germany for players. It wasn't that Germany's level of musical training had declined, but Karajan was in a position to get what he wanted, and he wanted the very best musicians, wherever they might be.

At this time Claire and I and our son, Stephen (aged two), were still living in Islington, at no. 25 Aberdeen Road. Our local pub, the Rising Sun, was a real musicians' hangout. One evening a friend of mine, the trombonist Martin Nicholls, told me that his wife, Antje, who was German, had seen an advertisement in a German magazine inviting musicians to apply for an audition with the Berlin Philharmonic. He copied the ad for me, and I took it to another friend, the harpsichordist Stanislav Heller, who helped me write my application letter in German. Stanislav lived across the street from me, and we had become very close friends.

I sent my application off and heard nothing for months. Then, just when I had started to think I never would hear anything, a letter came, instructing me to present myself at the Deutsches Museum in Munich (where the Berlin Phil was on tour) at twelve noon on January 29.

4

ICH WAR EIN BERLINER

THE SIX YEARS I SPENT WITH THE BERLIN Philharmonic were, without a doubt, the most interesting and musically formative years of my career in playing with orchestras. But they almost didn't happen. There's a famous story about this, which I have told before and others have written about. But it's too good not to tell again.

Months after applying for the post of solo flute, I received the letter from the Berlin Philharmonic, inviting me to audition for the job. I lost no time in buying my plane ticket. England was starting to bug me: this was the winter of 1968–1969, and there was constant industrial unrest; the post office had been on strike for a week.

Finally, audition day arrived. I made my way to Heathrow in good time, but the plane was late in taking off because of a snowstorm. As we approached Munich, I saw that it was snowing there, too. I looked down at the runway, with all the snow piled up, and I couldn't help thinking of the crash at this same airport, just eleven years earlier, in which the Manchester United football players were killed. Granted, their plane was trying to take off, not land, but the whole business did nothing to steady my nerves.

In fact, we did land safely, and I got a cab to take me to the museum where the auditions were to take place. I arrived at just about noon; however, I saw no indication of where the auditions were being held, and I had a hard time finding anyone to ask. Finally, I tracked down Dr. Wolfgang Stresemann, the orchestra's *Intendant* (general director). I introduced myself, but instead of welcoming me, he burst out, "But Mr. Galway! The audition has already taken place!"

I had heard of German efficiency, but how do you audition several flute players in five minutes? "But it's only five past twelve!" I replied.

"No, no!" he said excitedly. "*Nine* o'clock. We sent you a telegram. *Nine* o'clock!"

"I never received any telegram. The letter says *twelve*."

But Stresemann was adamant. In fact, he told me, they had heard wonderful flutists from all over Europe and had already chosen one.

"We'll pay your plane fare," Stresemann assured me. I reminded him that the plane fare was included in the invitation he had sent me, and he would have to pay that in any case.

But the plane fare wasn't the point. "Having come all this way," I blurted out, "at least I'd expect you to have the good manners to listen to me play the flute. How do you know I'm not better than any of the others?"

Whether he was afraid I might be right or was simply stung by the suggestion that he lacked good manners, Stresemann said, "Wait here," and stalked away. I took out my flute and played a few notes to make sure nothing had gone wrong in that quarter. A few minutes later, Stresemann reappeared and said, "Galway! Come and play. The Maestro will hear you."

I followed him into another room, where a pianist was seated on a platform. There was a large audience—the entire orchestra, I later learned, because all full members of the Berlin Philharmonic (that is, players who have passed their probationary year) vote on prospective new members.

I walked over to the pianist and handed him some music. The Ibert flute concerto was on top—I had just played it the day before at a BBC concert in Cardiff. (Jacques Ibert had written it expressly for Marcel Moyse in the thirties.)

"This isn't a piano audition," the pianist said. "Can you play a Mozart concerto?"

Well, I hadn't rehearsed any Mozart, but I said okay, and we began to play the first movement of the Mozart D Major Concerto. I found the pitch very high—I would learn that the pitch in Germany is always higher than in the United Kingdom—but I adjusted to it and played the first movement, complete with cadenza.

I had no time to think about how I was doing before a voice called out from the audience: "Now play *Daphnis and Chloe*." I didn't have the music, but fortunately I had studied it with John Francis and had played it not long before with Rozhdestvensky. Then this voice called again: "Play *L'Après-midi*." So I played it. "*Heldenleben*." So I did that—again, it had not been that long since I had played it with Zubin Mehta—and then the voice called for Brahms's Fourth. It occurred to me that it was pretty outrageous for this guy to force me to play all of the most difficult bits of the flute repertoire from memory. Orchestral players aren't normally expected to memorize, and if it hadn't been for John Francis's training, I probably wouldn't have been able to do it. Finally, the voice said, "Wait outside."

This peremptory treatment was beginning to get under my skin. Still, I did as I was told, and I was joined by the members of the orchestra who were still in their probationary period and not yet eligible to vote. We milled around, and some of them said encouraging things to me. Then Stresemann came back on the scene. "We want you to play again," he announced.

"Fine," I said, and followed him back into the concert hall.

This time, there were four other men with flutes on the platform; it turned out that two were from Germany, one was from Denmark, and one was from France. We were told to line up facing the audience, and Karajan called out—of course, the imperious voice had been his—"Now, from left to right, one after the other, play *A Midsummer Night's Dream.*" This time the music was supplied, and each of us played in turn. "Now Brahms's Fourth." Then *Heldenleben.* Then Karajan made us play the same things again, this time from right to left. "Wait outside!" he called, and then, "Thank you." Finally, a thank-you!

We didn't have to wait long. In a few minutes, Dr. Stresemann marched right up to me, grabbed my hand, and shook it vigorously. "Mr. Galway," he said grandly, "congratulations! You are now the principal flute with the Berlin Philharmonic. When can you start?"

"Listen here," I told him. "I don't know that I can start at all. I mean, I'm not sure that I *want* to start. Everybody's so rude here. You're all so rude that I don't feel I want to start. Since I got here, no one has said a kind word." While some of the younger players had been welcoming, I was put off completely by the arrogance of those in authority.

Stresemann looked as if he couldn't believe his ears. He said something about how it was the law in Germany that if you won an audition, you *had* to take the job. I pointed out that even if that was the law for Germans, it could hardly apply to a British subject.

"You cannot leave it like this," he said flatly.

"I'm sorry," I said. "I haven't time to stand around here arguing. I have a plane to catch. All I can say is that I'll think about it." With that, I said good-bye and headed to the front door to get a cab to the airport.

A few hours later I was back in London. I told Claire that I had been elected, and she merely said, "Oh, that's marvelous news," in a tone of voice that didn't suggest a high degree of excitement. But then I went to our local, the Rising Sun, and none of my musician friends had any doubts: I had to do it. The only person who was totally unimpressed was my mother. When I wrote to tell her that I would be joining the Berlin Philharmonic, she wrote back to say, "Oh dear, I do wish you'd come back to Belfast, get a nice job with the BBC orchestra here, and settle down."

In any case, I wrote back to Stresemann saying that I would give it a try for a month, but I wouldn't make any guarantees beyond that until I saw how things went. When I went back to Germany, though, everyone treated me like a returning hero. I signed on the dotted line and even agreed to the full probationary year.

I knew I had made the right choice the first time I actually played with the Berlin Philharmonic. The piece was Brahms's Second Symphony, and being inside that sound was like nothing I had ever experienced—not even with the LSO at its best.

I already regarded Herbert von Karajan as the emperor of conductors. In my ten years as a professional musician, I had played with some truly great ones, starting with Alex Gibson and going on to international stars like Davis, Mehta, Bernstein, and Rozhdestvensky. For me, though, Karajan topped them all.

In the first place, his understanding of the music was magnificent—and music of so many different types, from Bach to Mozart to Beethoven to Wagner to Verdi to Ravel. Karajan got down into the soul of the music, and, like Colin Davis, he wanted his players to get there, too, and to do much more than play the notes in the right order and at the right tempo. Karajan also wanted to meld us into a team, and he succeeded. All the different voices of our instruments formed one whole under his direction, and that whole expressed his vision of the music. If you watch him conducting—and there are some videos to be found on the Internet—you'll see that he doesn't merely beat time, he molds the phrases with his hands and brings the players along with him.

He was even willing to spend time working with individual players until they got it right. I remember once, when he was playing the harpsichord in one of the Brandenburg Concertos, he suddenly turned to me and said, "Jimmy, would you mind just playing it like this?" and he nearly hypnotized me into doing what he wanted. On another occasion, when he didn't like the tone of the violins, he stopped them and went to the piano and said, "Play this chord." The violins played the chord he had just played. "Now hold the note long." They did it again. "Right. Now softer." When they had done that, he said, "Now just begin the phrase like that." He would do this as often as he needed to, with as many players as he needed to.

That sort of thing is why he didn't like to guest-conduct at opera houses, where the production was someone else's. By the time I came to know him, he conducted opera only at the Salzburg Festival, where he could shape the production as he wished and personally coach the singers as well as the orchestra.

But I would be giving a false impression of him if I made it sound as if he treated us like automatons or chessmen. The overarching vision was his, and sometimes the smallest details, too. Yet he allowed his players a good deal of freedom to try things out in different ways, and if any of our experiments worked, he blended them into his conception, instead of making us do something that he had worked out ahead of time. Often, over the years, I've felt that the traditional way of playing certain passages was inferior, both instrumentally and musically. I tried to find my own way of playing them, and much of the time Karajan accepted what I had come up with.

Another element that went into Karajan's greatness was the orchestra he conducted. The Berlin Philharmonic had for a long time drawn the best players in Germany, and, as I've said, Karajan had recently started to cast his net throughout Europe. Quality attracts quality: young musicians who could have gone for first violin in any number of fine orchestras vied for a desk as second violin in Herbert's band. Having first-rate colleagues brings up everyone's level. Also, the money was tops—I believe that at the time, only the Metropolitan Opera in New York paid orchestral musicians better. So, all in all, I thought that being a part of the Berlin Philharmonic was one of the greatest things in the world.

George, Dad, and Mum. That's me behind Dad and Mum on a visit home from the Berlin Philharmonic in the early 1970s.

Berlin itself was something else again. To start with, I had a strong feeling that it was really very, very German. That may sound obvious, but I mean two things. First, that the city wasn't at all cosmopolitan. It has changed since then, but at the time, Berlin was very insular. Second, you could feel the shadow of the Third Reich when you saw the Brandenburg Gate and the Reichstag, which had been damaged first by the famous fire and then by Allied raids during the war and had been only partially rebuilt. I was a child of World War II, born three months after it started. Our first house, on Vere Street, was destroyed by the Luftwaffe when I was a year and a half old—not that I remember it firsthand, but I was told about it often enough. I had grown up thinking of Germany as an aggressive nation, and you could feel some of this quality when you looked at these remnants of the Third Reich. Of course, there were also wonderful things in Berlin, such as the Charlottenburg Palace in the far western part of the city, built by Frederick the Great's grandfather as a summer retreat for his wife, Sophie Charlotte. I loved to visit the palace and stroll in its beautiful garden.

Then there was the Wall—located within sight of our concert hall, the Philharmonie—and the strangeness of living in a divided city, with West Berlin existing as a sort of island ninety miles inside East Germany. We sometimes went across the Wall—which West Berliners could do, although East Berliners could not unless they were privileged characters. And being in East Berlin was the strangest experience of all.

Meanwhile, the first thing I had to do was find a flat. The problem was that I spoke hardly a word of German. I certainly couldn't have managed this on my own. I might have given up the job after all, except that a couple of the musicians who spoke some English stepped forward and befriended me. One was Johannes Mertens, the second flute. He had come up to me in Munich, the day of the audition, and said, "My name is Hans Mertens"—a touch of friendliness amid all of the "Come here" and "Do that" that had turned me off about the audition. Another was Siegfried Ceslick, a bass trombone player, who had a lovely wife, Helga, and a beautiful little girl. He showed me around Berlin a little and helped me look for an apartment. Then one day Helmut Nicolai, the first viola, came over and introduced himself as "Nick." He took over for Siegfried in showing me around, since Siegfried had less time because of his family responsibilities. Nick helped me find my first apartment, on Mommsenstrasse, over near the western end of the Tiergarten—the huge and beautiful park in the center of Berlin. Mommsenstrasse is basically straight across town from the Philharmonie, which is just south of the eastern end of the Tiergarten.

I quickly made friends with my upstairs neighbors at Mommsenstrasse, Uta and Reiner Gohring. She was a painter, he an engineer working on metal fatigue, and they became two of my best friends in Berlin.

Then there was Rainer Lafin. He was with the Radio Symphony Orchestra, and sometimes he played with me in the Berlin Philharmonic if we needed an extra flute. I had met him the very first week I was in Berlin, because he came to hear me play. We became very good friends and still are to this day.

One day Rainer asked me whether I'd like to go to visit Helmut Hammig. Hammig had been a famous flute maker in Germany before the war. But he unfortunately lived in the eastern part of Berlin, and after the war he got separated from the rest of the world by the Iron Curtain, and later the Berlin Wall.

We set a date for the excursion, and at the appointed time Rainer picked me up in his car and off we went toward the Wall. We had to drive across because at that time you couldn't take the train. Later, you could take a train that went along Friedrichstrasse.

We drove to Checkpoint Charlie, which was the only place where you could go through the Wall. And I do mean *through*: the Wall was so thick that Checkpoint Charlie was like a tunnel—totally surrealistic. Adding to the atmosphere were the border guards, who showed you exactly the meaning of the word *austere*. They examined our papers and eventually let us through. When we emerged into East

Berlin, it was even more surrealistic. Everything seemed in complete disrepair, and there were no people in sight. There were a lot of office buildings, and you had the feeling that people were inside working away like little moles, but you couldn't see anyone at the windows, and nobody was walking along the streets. Everything was gray.

Finally, we reached Hammig's house. Rainer and I had brought him a bottle of cognac, which, of course, you couldn't get in East Berlin—unless you knew somebody. We spent some time with Helmut that day, and for the rest of my stay in Berlin, we went back to visit him whenever we could manage it.

We talked about flutes and tried his flutes. I showed him my flutes, made by Mr. Cooper, which were the latest thing in flute building. Helmut was very interested in all of this, because, owing to his location, he wasn't able to keep up with what was going on in the flute world.

I must add that his flutes were very special instruments. Nowadays, you will still sometimes see a Helmut Hammig flute, and the person who owns it—like my friend Richard Taylor—owns it with pride and plays it with pride.

It was very sad to see how this great flute maker lived and to learn how the authorities treated him. I mean, here was Helmut Hammig, making, by hand, ten flutes a year, and these flutes were immediately taken by the government and sold. I don't know what sort of price they sold for, but the amount of money that was passed along to Helmut was barely enough to survive on, and he was living on the lowest level you can imagine.

When we left Helmut, we decided to go to a music shop nearby, because things were really cheap in East Berlin if you had Western money. Of course, there was next to nothing to buy, but if you *could* find something, it was cheap.

In fact, there wasn't much of interest to me. The shop didn't have any flute literature or orchestral studies for the flute. But I did buy one thing there, a book of orchestral extracts from the symphonies of Shostakovich—wouldn't you know?

Then we drove back to Checkpoint Charlie, and this time the guards *really* gave us a going-over, because they didn't want you smuggling people out. They searched the trunk and looked underneath the car with mirrors—it was like being in a James Bond movie.

Then, as we drove into West Berlin, all sorts of feelings awakened in me. We drove by the Gedächtniskirche, which had been a huge church at the eastern end of Kurfürstendamm. It had been mostly destroyed by Allied bombs during the war, with just one tower left standing. That tower remains there to this day, with a new church built alongside it. For me, seeing it brought to mind all the horrors of the war, all of the good people who died, in Germany as well as outside Germany, and all because of one mad, evil, egotistical Austrian. I couldn't help wondering what was going through the minds of Hitler's generals when they received orders from a man who really didn't know what he was doing. Take a person like Rommel, who was a very good soldier. It must have been a nightmare for him. If only someone had managed to shoot Hitler! But I guess he took good care to prevent that.

Then there was the present situation, as of 1970, with half of Berlin controlled by the Communists. I wondered, What would people from East Berlin think if they were able to come over to West Berlin and see the Ku'damm, as it's called—the main shopping street in Berlin. It had one shop after another, with the windows full of cameras or jewelry or mink coats. The contrast with the drabness and poverty of East Berlin would completely blow their minds.

But most East Berliners never had the chance to come over to West Berlin. At night the whole Wall was lit up, and there were guards with dogs patrolling it, up and down. If you tried to climb over the Wall, the guards would shoot you. It was unbelievable. Of course, you got used to it after a bit, and you stopped thinking about it. But this first visit to East Berlin really brought it home to me, and the whole experience awakened in me a hatred of Communism—of this system that treated its own people like slaves.

· · · · · · · ·

Soon Claire and little Stephen joined me in Berlin, but relations between Claire and me had been rocky, and the change of scenery didn't improve them. In some ways, they got worse. Claire had no interest in music—I'm not sure she ever came to a single concert I played in. And she certainly had no interest in listening to musicians talk shop, which is what I wanted to do as I started to learn a bit of German and make some friends among my colleagues. If I invited a few of the guys over to the flat to have a drink and talk about the performance, Claire simply went to bed. Also, there was the money question. I was making the best salary I had ever made in my life—big money indeed, by the standards of Carnalea Street. But Berlin was an expensive city to live in, and Claire always seemed to want more. Still, we staggered along for a while, as I settled into the routine of the Philharmonic's season.

This followed a pretty regular pattern, although there were variations year by year. The summer featured a tour, which always involved the Salzburg Festival and the Lucerne Festival and sometimes the Edinburgh Festival. Karajan was a freeman of the city of Lucerne, a great honor for someone who had not been born there and was not even Swiss. He could also be called the favorite son of Salzburg. In those days, the joke in Salzburg went, "This is where von Karajan was born. Oh, yes, and Mozart was born here, too."

Then we would return to Berlin for about two months before spending a week touring in the Federal Republic, as West Germany was officially known. Our concert hall, the Philharmonie, was (and is) a really outstanding building. The old concert hall had been destroyed by bombing during the war, and when life resumed afterward, the Berlin Philharmonic used various other halls as makeshift temporary homes. In 1955, when Karajan took over, he made plans for a new concert hall. It eventually opened in 1963, amid some controversy. It's very modern looking, gold-toned on the outside and pentagonal in shape on the inside. The members of the orchestra sat in tiers so that we could all see Karajan conducting, and the audience, also in tiers, surrounded the orchestra. The acoustics are terrific.

After our tour of West Germany, we went back to Berlin for the winter season, which included special concerts for Christmas and New Year's. Then in the spring we returned to Salzburg for the Salzburg Easter Festival. This was Karajan's brainchild, and he had started running it just two years before I joined the Philharmonic. It is a short festival, running ten days, and always includes an opera. After Salzburg, we went on a tour farther afield—elsewhere in Europe, or sometimes Japan or the United States.

When we traveled, we did it in style. It was the complete opposite of a tour of the States that the Royal Philharmonic did during my brief time with it, when we crisscrossed that great country in a bus, jouncing along uncomfortably and dying of boredom. No, with Karajan we did things right. Within Germany, we traveled in our own private train. It was blue and had a sign that read, "The Berlin Philharmonic Orchestra under the direction of Herbert von Karajan." Whenever we came to a station, the train slowed down, and the people of the town or village came out and waved to us. When we stopped for the night, we always stayed in the best hotels.

The Easter Festival my second year with the Philharmonic, 1970, was one of the absolute highlights of my orchestral life. The opera that year was *Götterdämmerung*, the last part of Wagner's *Ring*, and we had been working on it during the regular season in Berlin. We had also recorded the entire opera, with Karajan coaching the singers himself. Now, as I've mentioned, in my younger days I thought Wagner was a complete bore. When I visited Vienna with the London Junior Orchestra back in the fifties, I heard Karajan himself conduct *Rheingold*, the first part of the *Ring*. Or rather, I heard a few bars before I fell fast asleep. I woke up only during the applause at the end. Colin Davis's *Flying Dutchman* gave me my first inkling that Wagner was a really brilliant composer. But this *Götterdämmerung* in Salzburg blew me away. I was literally in tears at the end of the first night, and Wagner has never again been a closed book to me.

. . . .

As wonderful as my musical life was in those days, my private life was not. Claire and I grew more and more out of tune with each other, and finally I just came home one evening and said, "I think we ought to pack it in. I think I want a divorce."

Claire didn't argue with me about the divorce, but she immediately turned to financial matters—with some justification, I have to say in retrospect. At the time, though, I shouted, "Okay, if you want our house in London, you can have my share. Have it all! I don't really need it and I don't want it and it doesn't mean anything to me." I grabbed a piece of paper and wrote something down, assigning the house to her. I then went to Uta and Reiner and asked whether I could stay with them until Claire moved out. Of course, they said yes, but they didn't have a lot of space, so I spent a few nights sleeping on the floor in a little room behind their kitchen.

Once Claire and Stephen left, I moved back to my own flat, but I found that I didn't really like eating dinner alone, nor did I want to expend the effort to cook for myself every night. So I suggested a deal with Uta, which she accepted, namely, that I would cook one night and she would cook the next. Eventually, we told others in the building—it was mostly a young crowd, some of them still students—and gradually we got about fifteen people enrolled in our scheme. In fact, the place became almost a sort of commune, except that each person or family had their own flat.

The others were very helpful about letting me juggle my turns to cook so as to fit the Philharmonic's schedule. I remember one time I made Irish stew, which most of them had never tasted before, and it was a big hit. Eventually, the arrangement fell apart—a couple of members fell down on the job and didn't get dinner on the table on their assigned night, and others decided to pull out. But it was great while it lasted.

Meanwhile, associating with those kids broadened my musical horizons in a different direction from Herr Wagner. They were all

Still practicing, in my days with the Berlin Philharmonic.

deeply into pop music, and I found myself listening to it with them. A lot of it was junk, of course, but I found that some of it was really good. The Beatles, for example, were producing some tremendous music. I also spent a lot of time listening to Frank Zappa and Pink Floyd. I got a real kick out of Frank Zappa's beard—in fact, I liked it so much that I started to grow one just like it. You can imagine Karajan's expression when he first saw it.

Then I carried things a step further. I had always had a rebellious streak, and the starchy German society of that time probably did something to arouse it. Anyway, once you have a Frank Zappa beard, it would seem rather silly to wear a jacket and tie. So I started turning up for rehearsals and even performances in quite casual clothes. At some point I bought a leather jacket, which was not quite respectable in those days. The first time I wore it to the Philharmonie, one of the guys called out, "Hey, here's our rocker!" and that became my nickname: "the Berlin Phil's rocker." One day Karajan was heard to say, "Talking to Jimmy Galway is like talking to a man from Mars."

By this time, Karajan had started to branch out: besides concerts and recordings, the Philharmonic was doing special television broadcasts and even films. Because of all the equipment needed for the films, we mostly didn't do them in the Philharmonie itself. Instead, we went to a place that seemed to be an old warehouse. It was very spartan; no one had bothered to fit it up properly, so there were no dressing rooms. Or rather, there was one dressing room: Karajan himself had a bizarre round white object that looked like a bathysphere, and that was where he changed clothes. Meanwhile, the rest of us had to put up with an open area, with nowhere to lock things away.

Karajan had decided that we had to wear tails for these films, so there was no question of not changing clothes. One day—I remember that we were filming the Beethoven symphonies—I hung up my gear, including my prized Italian leather jacket. But when I came back to change, it was gone. So I had to go home on the bus wearing my tails.

Now, whoever stole my gear had taken my keys out of the jacket pocket and hung them up on the little peg. So I thought at first that it was one of the trumpet players pulling my leg, and I figured he would bring my stuff back the next day. When that didn't happen, I asked the trumpeters about it, and they all said, "No, no, Jimmy, it's not us."

I went to Karajan's assistant, the one who had set up the film sessions, and I explained the situation.

"Well, I'm not responsible," he said.

I said, "Well, neither am I. It's like this: you expect us to leave our stuff there, and it's not safe. If you want me to go back, you've got to pay me the money that jacket cost." I think it was about eight hundred deutsche marks, maybe a thousand—anyway, it was not cheap.

He hemmed and hawed a bit, and we left it hanging, because there wasn't another session actually booked. Then they wanted to do a shot of five flutes for the Eroica Symphony. I said, "I can't go there, because there's nowhere safe to leave your stuff." Karajan's assistant still argued, but eventually he admitted that he was in the wrong, and management paid for my jacket.

Meanwhile, I had discovered that despite Berlin's middle-class starchiness, the city had a lively restaurant scene. It had plenty of bars, too, and with the exception of Karajan himself, my fellow musicians were as eager as those in every other orchestra I had played in to unwind after a performance by hoisting a few. Between the food and the drink, my weight got up to fourteen stone—nearly two hundred pounds. And I'm no six-footer. The beer-barrel body topped with all that hair was quite a sight.

Unfortunately, Karajan thought so, too. He decreed that I could not appear in any broadcast, film, or even still photograph. If I was playing in that performance, the cameraman had to avoid me. This really needled me. Now, of course, I realize that he was right: there is a certain respect owed to an institution like the Philharmonic, and

I wasn't showing it. But at the time, it seemed that he was simply taking his revenge on me because I flouted the conventional rules.

Mind you, none of this affected my actual playing. I wasn't practicing as hard as I did when I was a kid or when I first joined the LSO and felt that I had so much catching up to do. But I practiced as much as I needed to in order to stay in top form. And however late I had been out the night before, if there was a rehearsal or a recording session scheduled for 10 a.m., as happened on most days, I was in my place and ready to go.

Speaking of recordings, we did some marvelous ones during my time with the Berlin Philharmonic. We recorded all nine Beethoven symphonies, and we did a few operas, such as *Fidelio* with Jon Vickers and *La Bohème* with Pavarotti (although to my sorrow I missed the stage performance of *La Bohème*, for reasons I shall relate later). When Pavarotti came walking in, Karajan introduced him to us as the Weltmeister. This is German for "world champion boxer," and that's how Karajan meant it—Pavarotti was the absolute champion. When Pavarotti started to sing, the orchestra members couldn't believe it. He just blew us away. He was so nice to work with, too, and he and Karajan had a great relationship.

That *Bohème* recording was done at the Jesus-Christus-Kirche in Dahlem, a posh suburb in southwestern Berlin. The building had a marvelous sound. To this day, when I hear a recording of the Berlin Philharmonic, I can tell where it was recorded. We did the Schumann symphonies there and "Salome's Dance" from the Richard Strauss opera. And we recorded two of the big Bruckner symphonies. I had never played them before in my life, and I was just amazed at these great pieces. Equally amazing was the sound of the orchestra and how everyone attacked this music. It wasn't simply people playing some notes. The musicians seemed to be speaking from within.

Karajan recorded a lot of things twice or three times over the years— not because he had drastically changed his conception of the pieces, but because the techniques of recording were constantly improving, and the sound was so much better. He wanted to be represented in the newest technology—FFRR, stereophonic, whatever. He was very much interested in the technical side of things. When Karajan sat in the recording booth, it was all the technicians could do to stop him from fiddling around with the knobs and changing the balance.

We had some wonderful guest soloists and guest conductors with the Berlin Philharmonic. I've mentioned my first encounter with Slava Rostropovich, as he is fondly known in the music business, at Carnegie Hall when I was with the LSO. The first time I played with him in the Philharmonic, it was the Dvořák Cello Concerto, conducted by Karajan. That concerto has a big part for the flute. I knew the piece very well—it was popular in England, and we'd played it a lot—and I really enjoyed it. At the end, Rostropovich put his cello down on the stage and came walking through the orchestra. I thought, This is a riot—he doesn't even know how to get off the stage. In fact, he knew exactly where he was going. He walked over to me, pulled me to my feet, and kissed me on the lips. I was startled, to say the least, but then I learned that he kissed everybody that way—there was no kissing on the cheek for Slava.

Another great soloist we had was Yehudi Menuhin. By the time I was in Berlin, he was no longer technically that great—he was not the Menuhin I remembered from my childhood, when he recorded the Elgar Concerto, conducted by no less than Sir Edward Elgar. Nevertheless, Menuhin was still a wonderful musician, and he had charisma. Everyone loved him. He sometimes came at Christmas and played pieces like a Brandenburg Concerto, and that was always a grand occasion. I remember very well the time he played the Beethoven Violin Concerto, which is one of the most difficult pieces. For the first time ever in the Philharmonie, we had people sitting on the stairs. This was not allowed, because of the fire department, and I don't know how they got in there, but they did. The slow movement was *so* beautiful, and the people just adored him.

We often had guest conductors, and we had some jolly moments with them, though I'm afraid we didn't always treat them very well. Karajan kept us on such a short chain that if he wasn't on the podium, we kicked up our heels during rehearsals, and it was a bit hard on the visiting conductors. There was Eugen Jochum, for example. He was wonderful, and I really enjoyed playing the big Bruckner symphonies with him. But we used to tease him something terrible. When we acted up, he would call out: "Gentlemen, gentlemen, please—come on." We'd behave ourselves for a little bit, but then we'd start the whole process all over again. He would threaten to leave, but we always begged, "Herr Professor, please don't leave." Eventually, we got through the rehearsal alive, and the performances were always top-drawer.

Interestingly, the Berlin Philharmonic never brought over any of the really prominent young American conductors while I was there—people like Lorin Maazel or Leonard Slatkin or Leonard Bernstein. It was a very German type of orchestra, very European, so everyone who got asked to conduct was European. We often had Rozhdestvensky, for example, and there was a Croatian conductor named Lovro Matačić. I remember Matačić beating time on his chest, and he had a very hairy chest. But I enjoyed playing for him—he was a real character.

Speaking of Eugen Jochum, I should mention the first girl to sit in the flute section of the Berlin Philharmonic, a young lady named Roswitha Stäge. Some of the self-governing orchestras, like the Berlin Philharmonic and the London Symphony, were much slower to take in women than were orchestras run by outside boards. Whether the men really believed that woman musicians would adversely affect the sound, I don't know. At any rate, Roswitha was a student of mine and a very good flutist. She was one of the first women to play in the Berlin Philharmonic. Actually, the second harp at that time was a woman, but she was married to the first harp, so people thought that didn't count.

The first time Roswitha played in the orchestra with me, she was so excited. She didn't have a solo, but simply to be there as a full member of the Berlin Philharmonic was a real triumph. The next day the critics wrote mostly about her and not about the wonderful guest conductor, Mr. Jochum.

. . . .

After I broke up with Claire, I started dating various girls, but nothing clicked. Then one day I went to a concert of modern music at the Akademie der Künste, the modern-art center of Berlin. Most of the people in the audience were taking the music very seriously, but I found it unintentionally hilarious. I had a sense that the very pretty girl sitting behind me found it as funny as I did. One piece, for example, was called "The Sinking of the *Titanic*," and that's what it sounded like. In addition to a violin and some other conventional instruments, there was also a circular saw, and the violinist occasionally stopped playing and started to ring bells. When it was over, I turned and said to the girl, "This is rubbish, isn't it?" She didn't reply, but she smiled.

At the end of the performance, I turned to her again and said, "You shouldn't worry about this sort of rubbish, you know. Come and hear some good flute playing sometime."

She surprised me by asking whether I knew a flutist named Peter-Lukas Graf. I did, and I could honestly say that he was terrific. He's about ten years older than I am; he had studied with Marcel Moyse at the Paris Conservatoire and had gone on to a great international career. It turned out that the girl, whose name was Annie Renggli, knew him well from her hometown of Lucerne, where he had played with the Festival Orchestra. So my knowing him, too, helped break the ice.

Annie and I saw each other several times over the next few days, and I learned that she had been trying to decide whether to marry her boyfriend back home. Her mother had sent her on a trip to Berlin to sort things out. By the time I put her on the train back to Lucerne, the boyfriend was out of the picture. Annie told me later that the first thing her mother said after catching sight of her was "Listen, Annie, are you in love or something?"

We were married on May 2, 1972, at the lovely little church in Platten, along Lake Zurich. Peter-Lukas Graf—P-Luke, we called him—played at the wedding. We moved into an apartment on

Mommsenstrasse just down the street from the building where I had lived during my first three years in Berlin. It was a great flat with two big balconies. In fact, it was so large that one Christmas we invited the entire Berlin Philharmonic over. They brought their instruments and played Beethoven's Eighth for the neighbors.

Being married to Annie calmed me down considerably, to Karajan's great relief. I even had my hair and beard trimmed for the wedding. The birth of our son, Patrick (Paddy), also helped steady me. For a couple of years, everything went along fine. From the outside, it must have looked as if I were fitting into the Berlin Philharmonic mold.

The fact remained, however, that I was still an orchestral player. Karajan sometimes gave me a concerto or a shorter piece in which I was featured, but mostly my flute was heard for only a few bars before the rest of the orchestra came crashing in on me. What happened then could be described as something like a corkscrew going into a cork. I was the cork, and the Berlin Philharmonic was the bottle. The corkscrew was my ambition to be a soloist. It turned slowly at the beginning, then picked up speed, and finally—pop!—out I came.

It began with my taking on outside gigs—solos and chamber music, mostly in England. This was very satisfying artistically, but it proved a strain in terms of time and money. Many of the gigs paid quite well, but I had to provide my own transportation, and flying from Berlin to London wasn't cheap. Also, if the Philharmonic was performing or rehearsing on any day that I was away, my salary was docked accordingly.

One friend to whom I confided some of my ambitions was Lindsay Armstrong, the manager of the New Irish Chamber Orchestra. Once when I was in Dublin, playing with his group, he said, "Why don't you get yourself an agent, Jimmy?"

I shot back, "Agents! They're all a bunch of sharks."

Lindsay dropped the subject, but a few days later I got a letter from someone I had never heard of, named Michael Emmerson. He wrote, "Dear Jimmy, I hear you have a very low opinion of agents as a race and I would like to put this right. Why don't you call and see me sometime?"

I wasn't inclined to do this, but a few weeks later I happened to be in London, and I thought, Why not?

I went to see him and liked him immediately. We set up an arrangement, and right away, my bookings increased, and with them my income from that source. But, as I said, that meant a decrease in income from the Berlin Philharmonic. One day I mentioned this to Michael, and he shot back, "Jimmy, if you're ever going to make it, you'll have to leave the Berlin Philharmonic."

I was stunned. I had always wanted to be a soloist, going back to my student days in London. But to actually leave the Berlin Philharmonic and say good-bye to the security it offered? You know, when you are hired by an outfit like the Berlin Philharmonic or the Metropolitan Opera, you go in there in the morning and you come out fifty years later. People simply don't leave until they're ready to go out to pasture. Michael and I hashed it backward and forward for two whole days before he finally convinced me that I could never make it big if I didn't take the plunge.

Then I flew back to Berlin and put the case to Annie. The first thing she said was, "Do you think it's safe?" After all, she was the mother of one small child, with twins on the way, and she had to think of them. She pointed out, as I had heard so many times before, that people didn't expect to go to a flute recital the way you would go to a piano or violin recital. Could I think of any flutist except Jean-Pierre Rampal who had really made it as a soloist?

But I insisted, "I've got to do this, Annie. I've really got to get it together."

Finally, I went to Karajan himself. I broke the news that I had decided to leave the orchestra, and I explained why.

I had been afraid he would explode, but instead he replied very seriously, "Fine, Jimmy. You leave the orchestra if you feel you have something really worth doing. If you feel you must do something, do it. When I was a youngster, there were things I didn't do that I thought I should have done and later regretted them. And I wouldn't want you to be in the same situation."

I do think he meant what he said, with at least part of his mind and heart. But he didn't take it so calmly when he saw that I really did intend to leave.

In August 1974, I handed in a written letter of resignation, to take effect at the end of the season. This time Karajan did explode. A little while later, Lothar Koch came up to me. He was first oboe, which meant that he was the guy who sat to my left. He told me that Herbert had said to him, "Go and be nice to Jimmy and try to get him to stay in the orchestra."

I said to Lothar, "There's no point in being nice to me. It has nothing to do with people being nice to me or not being nice to me. I simply want to do something else. I want to leave and do something else, and that's all there is to it."

Relations with Karajan were frosty from then on, and they took a turn for the worse during our tour in New York that fall. I asked for leave to return to Berlin because Annie was expecting our twins any day. Karajan refused, and I fumed. I rang Annie to tell her, and when she said she was just about to go to the hospital, I told her I'd be there as soon as I could. I threw my belongings into my bags and ran downstairs, where I saw my friend Helmut Nicolai. I called out, "Hey, Nick, can you pay my bill at the hotel? Annie is just off to the hospital and I'm heading to the airport." (As it happens, Nick eventually also left the Berlin Philharmonic; he moved on to the Munich Philharmonic, to work with the eccentric but brilliant Sergiu Celibidache.)

I arrived at the hospital in time for the birth of our daughters, Charlotte and Jennifer, which I actually witnessed. I believe it wasn't that common in those days for the husband to be present, at least not in Germany, but I found it an amazing experience, watching first one and then the other little creature emerge into the world.

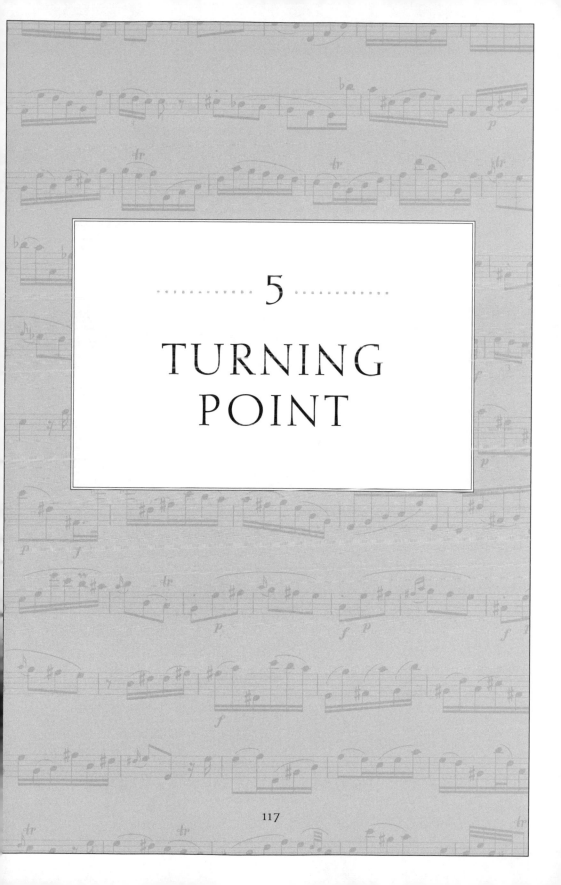

5

TURNING
POINT

I RESUMED MY PLACE AS FIRST FLUTE WHEN THE orchestra returned to Berlin, but I did not withdraw my resignation, and relations with Karajan didn't improve. They took another sharp turn for the worse in March, just a few days before we were due to leave for Salzburg for the Easter Festival. We were rehearsing *La Bohème* in preparation for Salzburg.

There had been a pause in the rehearsal, and I took the opportunity to explain something to the second flute. While I was still talking, Karajan spoke to me, and I asked him to wait a second while I fixed a problem in the flute section. Well, you never ask Karajan to wait for anything. I had crossed the boundary of acceptable behavior.

Nothing happened right away. Karajan went on with the rehearsal. However, a few minutes after it had finished, a member of the orchestra committee came over to me. The committee acts as liaison between the players and management, passing on information and settling problems. In this case, it was information: Karajan would prefer that I not go to Salzburg with the others.

That really hurt. First, that he would go that far to punish me for a pretty mild form of back talk (although, of course, I think he was actually punishing me for not withdrawing my resignation). Second, I would miss doing *La Bohème* with Pavarotti, which I had been greatly looking forward to. And third, this hit me badly in the pocket. The Salzburg festivals paid very well. In fact, we had already received some of the fee in advance, and I had to give it all back.

The silver lining, however, was that it gave me time to go to London and make two recordings for RCA. These two recordings, which became famous in the classical-music world, were a major turning point in launching my solo career. One was with Martha Argerich; it is a very fine classical flute and piano disk, with sonatas by Prokofiev and César Franck. To this day, I think it's probably the best recording of these two works. Playing with Martha was a great event for me. I went to her house near Geneva, and we rehearsed both pieces in preparation for the recording, which we did in the famous Kingsway Hall in London.

The other record was called *Showpieces for Flute* (it was reissued a few years later as *Man with the Golden Flute*). I did that recording with Charles Gerhardt conducting the National Philharmonic Orchestra, and, as the title implies, it features a lot of virtuoso flute music, which was fun but very strenuous to play. It contains the famous Paganini "Moto Perpetuo," which I did in one breath, or so everyone was led to believe. In fact, we recorded it in bits and put it all together with the help of editors and a good razor blade. In those days, everything was recorded on tape, and, yes, the editing was done with a razor blade. There was an ongoing joke about the best parts of a recording lying on the floor.

It had been just a short time before this that I had met the pianist Phillip Moll, who is still with me after all these years. How this came about is that during an audition for a flute position with the Berlin Philharmonic, I asked the pianist to play a bit softer, because we were having difficulty hearing the contestants. As I mentioned earlier, when auditions were held for the Berlin Phil, the entire orchestra

Hanging around backstage in Japan with the indispensable Phillip Moll.

and Karajan attended and voted right then and there. When I complained about the pianist playing too loud, Karajan turned to me and told me to get in touch with Phillip Moll, who was working at the Deutsche Oper at the time.

I did get in touch with Phillip and I heard him play, so I knew he was the one I wanted to coach me for *Showpieces*. This coaching was in the form of our playing the material through together several times to see where the weak points were. This also helped me build up the stamina that was required for this sort of recording, especially because we wanted to get it done as quickly as we could. Playing solo is quite different from being a member of an orchestra and requires much more preparation. The task was made more difficult by the amount of work I had to do with the Philharmonic during that period. Finding the time to learn and practice these pieces was a major endeavor, but playing them all through with Phillip showed me the places where I would have to concentrate and practice the hardest to bring them to perfection.

It was through these sessions in my apartment at Mommsenstrasse no. 50 that Phillip and I got to know each other. We formed a life-long friendship and partnership. Phillip and I enjoyed playing these little pieces, and we play them in concert to this day. We have done hundreds of recitals together since those early days.

I would like to add that this recording was inspired by Jascha Heifetz, who is my all-time hero on the violin. He had made many recordings of charming little virtuoso pieces, and this is what sparked the idea for our record. The only difference was that I did them with an orchestra, whereas Heifetz did them with the piano. My thought was that people had heard flute and piano records before, and I wanted to present something different.

Meanwhile, my contract with the Berlin Philharmonic still had another couple of months to run. I went back to Berlin after the recording sessions and took my place again—but only when there was a guest conductor. If Karajan was conducting, I was told to stay away. I was amazed that Karajan, who thought I was the best flute player he had ever had, would ban me from playing. It was a sad time for me, but I got over it by immersing myself in the new direction my career was taking. The last piece I played with the Berlin Philharmonic was Mussorgsky's *Pictures at an Exhibition*, conducted by Claudio Abbado.

A year or so later, I went to the Salzburg Festival and met Karajan. We found that we were back on speaking terms, though we did not mention the scene at the Philharmonie. He was very nice to me, and in fact, without exactly apologizing, he indicated that he knew that he, too, had not behaved very well. He congratulated me on selling nearly a million records since I'd left the Berlin Philharmonic. We remained friendly after that—but, sadly, I never played for him again.

It was in July 1975 that I left the Berlin Philharmonic, and a few days later we moved to Lucerne, where Annie's mother had found us a lovely apartment with a view of the lake. Not that I had a lot of time to enjoy it. In that first year out on my own, I did well over a hundred concerts in England and elsewhere, and I played with all the major London orchestras. Some of these concerts were quite a gift to the promoters, I was paid so little. But at the time we were just happy to have concerts and get the message out there. This is part of building a career. You don't simply go from being a member of the orchestra one day to filling the Royal Albert Hall as a soloist the next. It's not like that. You have to do a lot of touring and play smaller venues to build up your reputation so that people want to come and hear you.

I often played with an outfit called the London Virtuosi—in fact, this was one of the groups I had flown to England to do chamber gigs with when I was still with the Berlin Philharmonic. It was basically a string quartet and an oboe—plus the flute when I was there. It was led by John Georgiadis, who was also the solo violin and leader of the London Symphony, and by my oboist friend Anthony Camden, whom I had met on my very first day at the Royal College. Anthony and I remained lifelong friends—indeed, I recently had the sadness of watching him die, from one of those horrible diseases that affect the nervous system.

Besides Anthony and John, there was Roger Lord on the viola, Moray Welsh on the cello, and David Lumsden on the harpsichord. David later became the principal of the Royal Academy, and Moray had studied with Rostropovich in Russia. They were all very good players. We did pieces like the Bach sonatas and a Telemann quartet. We got on TV once with the Telemann, and I remember the TV people scratching their heads over the fact that six people were playing a quartet. Tony Curtis was also on this show to do a segment with people from a town in England called Ugly. The TV producers had gone to this village and persuaded several people with odd-shaped noses to come on the show and compare noses with Tony Curtis, who was well known for his classic profile. Curtis, incidentally, plays the flute. He told me Frank Sinatra had given him a gold flute. Nice to have friends like that.

I enjoyed doing concerts around England with these guys. Then one time we did a tour of Ireland, and that was a riot. I was becoming fairly well known by that time, so instead of using the name London Virtuosi, we billed ourselves as the Galway Flute Quartet. Only afterward did it occur to us that people were likely to think we were four flute players from County Galway.

In the course of this tour, we went all the way up to the northern tip of County Donegal. One day John and Roger decided to take advantage of the situation and play a game of golf at the course in Greencastle, which is apparently quite highly regarded. Moray and I went along for the walk. At one point John threw out the challenge that we couldn't hit the ball if we tried. So I bet him my fee for the evening that I could hit the ball. I was pretty confident I could. Well, I took a swipe at it, and it fell off the tee, but it didn't go anywhere. John said that didn't count, but I pointed out that if I hadn't hit the ball, it would still be on the tee. As it was lying on the ground, technically I had hit it.

Then I offered to double the wager. I said, "Okay, I'll hit it into the sea next time"—since the golf course overlooks the Atlantic Ocean. I took another swipe, and I think I dug up half the golf course along with the ball. But that whole clump of ball and dirt and grass did indeed go over the cliff into the sea.

Of course, there was no talking to John after that. He was so annoyed at having to pay this money out to a nongolfer. But we did have wonderful times, and the music making was great.

The most amazing experience that first summer was returning to the Proms. I had been back only once before, with the Berlin Phil, since I'd played there with Sir Malcolm Sargent nearly ten years earlier. As I mentioned, I had had the pleasure of playing "The Sailor's Hornpipe" with Sir Malcolm in the famous Last Night of the Proms. Now, coming back as a full-fledged soloist, I was asked to play the Mozart Concerto in D at the Albert Hall.

My one disappointment was that they were going to televise the second half of the concert, and I was in the first half. I needed to be seen on TV, and my manager had had some T-shirts made with the logo "The Man with the Golden Flute."

It had become widely known that when I was still a member of the Berlin Philharmonic, I had begun to use a 14-karat gold flute, made for me by Albert Cooper of London. The name the "Man with the Golden Flute" has stuck with me to this day (as the title of this book bears witness). A lot of people have asked me whether I ever get tired of it, and the answer is simply, "No!" After Jean-Pierre Rampal, I was the flute player who put gold flutes on the market. Many professional flutists now play gold instruments, and it is not uncommon these days for a teenage student to turn up for a lesson with a fine gold instrument.

In any case, as I approached the Albert Hall that evening, I saw a bunch of Prommers, most of them young, wearing our T-shirts. When we started the performance, these kids' reaction to the Mozart was just exhilarating. During the first movement, they bounced along as I played the more difficult bits in the concerto. Then in the slow movement, they calmed down and simply let the music wash over them. I realized how much I had missed the wonderful, crazy atmosphere of the Proms.

I finished the first half and watched the second half on TV, and, to my delight, right in the front row were all these kids wearing our T-shirts. So we got our publicity despite my not performing in the second half.

I still wasn't sure, though, that the whole thing was going to work—that is, that I could really make a living as a soloist—so when I was offered a professorship at the Eastman School of Music in Rochester, New York, I accepted. This deal was set up with Robert Freeman, the dean of the school. We had lunch at the infamous Watergate Hotel in Washington, D.C. In a verbal contract, Bob, as he became known to me, told me I could do whatever I wanted regarding time off for my career. Sadly, this did not go according to plan. I think Bob assumed that I would occasionally take a day off and go to New York City for a quick recording session and be back the following day. He was not expecting me to go traipsing all over Europe like a wandering minstrel for five weeks and then return for a week or two before going off to Japan to play a recital tour. As you can imagine, it did not work out at all, and I had to quit at the end of my first semester.

Besides playing in all sorts of venues in Britain and Europe, I found a toehold in the United States. I had played in America before, of course, with the LSO, the Royal Philharmonic, and the Berlin Philharmonic. But that was only as a member of the band. My first U.S. engagement as a soloist came about through my old connection with Ernest Fleischmann.

Ernest had been a big fan of mine at the LSO. He liked my playing and appreciated my attitude—the fact that I just came along and played and tried to avoid getting caught in the cliquishness and bickering that went on in the orchestra. After he left the LSO, he went to the United States and became the managing director of the Los Angeles Philharmonic and the Hollywood Bowl. So when I began my solo career, my management, which was called London Artists at the time, got in touch with Ernest, because he knew what I could do. He was the only person in America who did know, at that point. He arranged for me to perform at the Hollywood Bowl, that great amphitheater in the hills above Los Angeles, on three consecutive nights in the summer of 1976. I think I played everything I knew with the Bowl orchestra—the Brandenburg Concertos, flute concertos, and a bunch of other things. This was my first solo exposure in the United States, and it was a big hit.

Another high point of that period was playing for Queen Elizabeth and Prince Philip. It happened on November 23, 1976, at the Royal Concert for Saint Cecilia's Day at the Albert Hall. I was playing the Mozart Concerto for Flute and Harp with the great Spanish harpist Marisa Robles. (Her professional debut, twenty years earlier, had been in this same piece, with Jean-Pierre Rampal.) It went very well. The audience gave us a standing ovation, which is not that common in the Royal Albert Hall.

During the interval following the concerto, Marisa and I were led to a small room outside the royal box and introduced to Her Majesty and His Royal Highness. I'm not often at a loss for words, as you may have noticed, but in the presence of the queen I suddenly was. That's a condition she encounters frequently, however, and she had long ago learned how to ask a question that would get her guest talking. In my case, she asked me whether Mozart was difficult to play. I explained that most of his works were not technically difficult, but that it could be hard to find the right style to play them in.

That was the first time I played for the queen, but I'm glad to say it was not the last. It is always a great pleasure to play for her, as she brings something very special to every event she attends.

I then made a highly successful tour of South Africa, Australia, and Japan. I was fortunate enough on the second and third legs of

I am still traveling, here conducting in Istanbul in 2002.

this trip to be working with Hiroyuki Iwaki, a very good Japanese conductor. Iwaki was also the principal conductor of the Melbourne Symphony. I knew him because he had guest-conducted the Berlin Philharmonic several times when I was still with Herbert's band. I had always played for him when he was our guest in Berlin.

I could hardly believe the reception I got in those far-flung places. The applause was like nothing I had ever heard. Even more amazing was the day when a man came up to me on the street in Japan and said, "You know, I heard your concert in Cape Town as well, and I'll never forget it."

One way and another, my career was falling into place. During the first two years after I left the Berlin Philharmonic, I toured more than twenty countries, made six records, and did a lot of TV appearances. I was asked to teach master classes in England and Scotland, which I did. And then, after I had played in the Lucerne Festival, I was asked to teach a master class there, in my adopted hometown. That is when my life as I had known it almost came to an end.

It was August of 1977, and Marcel Moyse, who had become a very good friend, was teaching his own master class in the town of Boswil, between Lucerne and Zurich. One day I invited the kids in my class to come along with me and pay him a visit. Phillip Moll, who was assisting with my class, gave me a ride (I had never learned to drive a car, and I still haven't), and the students found their own means of transport. We convened in Boswil, and the young flutists got to meet the master and hear him teach. Sadly, however, they did not get to hear him play, as his playing days were over.

After the session, I spent a little time talking privately with Marcel and then decided to walk to a nice restaurant that I knew nearby. On the way, I ran into several of my pupils, who were also heading for dinner, and we were quite a good little group strolling along the road—until the motorbike came along. I heard this bike from some way off and told the kids not to walk in the road. We all left the road for the safety of a little patch of green grass, and as the motorbike came around the corner it left the road and headed straight toward us.

We never found out how the rider lost control of his vehicle, but he plowed into us at full speed, hitting first one of the boys, then one of the girls, and then me, throwing me into the air. I knew immediately that something was very wrong with both of my legs; it wasn't until later that I learned I also had a broken arm. It was here that I found out the meaning of being knocked out of your shoes. They had disappeared, and there I was lying in the middle of the road. Fortunately, I still had my wits about me and was able to crawl to the side of the road. I had no sooner reached the safety of the little grass bank when a car came speeding along without even slowing down. I guess the driver was completely unaware of what had just taken place.

This is a story that I've told before and do not particularly want to relive again in any detail. Suffice it to say that I spent four months in a hospital, much of it in traction and feeling pretty sorry for myself—justifiably, I thought. Near the end of the third month, when I thought I was about to be released, the surgeon, Professor Bruno Vogt, gave me the news that my legs weren't knitting straight, and he would need to operate. Recovering from the operation was no picnic, but at least the surgery worked, and after another month in the hospital, I was finally sent home in a wheelchair, three days before Christmas. I became friends with Professor Vogt, and by chance I am now his neighbor in Meggen, the little village where I live in Switzerland.

Amid the misery and boredom of hospital life, there were some bright spots. The first was that our old friend P-Luke Graf went into action as soon as he heard about the accident. He got me transferred from the little hospital near Boswil to the main hospital in Lucerne, where Professor Vogt practiced. I learned that Vogt was one of the leading orthopedists in Switzerland—a country renowned for its orthopedists. I frequently thanked God that I was under Professor Vogt's care. Without him, I probably would have needed a wheelchair for the rest of my life.

For that matter, it was the accident that brought me back to belief in God. I had been quite religious as a boy, but during my Berlin years, I had somehow drifted away. Yet as I lay there in bed, I found myself thinking, "It's a good thing that last concert I had was really great, because it would have been terrible if I'd died and people had said, 'You know, that last concert wasn't any good anyway.'" However, I didn't die, and that last concert really *was* great, and that made me think, "I'm here for a reason. And there's got to be a higher power behind this whole thing." This led me back to believing in God and Jesus Christ.

Now, I was aware that you have various choices; belief in a higher power can take many different forms. But if you want to believe in something where a miracle really happened and was seen to happen by people at the time—well, that thought drew me back to the biblical Christianity of my youth. And that gave me a different outlook on everything. Because there I was, getting another chance—another chance to prove my talent, to thank God for my talent.

Another bright spot, which was more mundane but also a very good thing, was that I resolved to use this time when I wasn't touring to lose the rest of the extra weight I was still carrying from my Berlin days. I had gotten rid of some of it by running and playing tennis, but I was still too heavy. So I went on a strict diet—porridge for breakfast and a vegetarian lunch, which Annie brought from home every day. By the time I was released from the hospital, I was back to the weight I should have been.

It was also while I was in the hospital that I discovered a song that became very important to me—another turning point, you might say, in my career. This came about when Madeleine Kasket—the PR woman for RCA, whom I had met during our recording sessions—flew over from London for a visit and brought me some cassettes by the American composer and singer John Denver. She thought I would

When Jeanne and I were on tour in Japan in 2005, our good friend (and former president of Rolex Japan) Chris McDonald (between myself and Jeanne) arranged a gathering after a concert in Suntory Hall in Tokyo. To my right is His Imperial Highness Tomohito of Mikasa, a cousin of the Emperor of Japan.

appreciate them, and she was right—I liked them all. But what really struck me was the coincidence that Denver had written perhaps the most beautiful of these songs for his wife and called it "Annie's Song." By that time, I was able to practice a little, so I knew that I could still play the flute. I decided that I would have to record "Annie's Song" when I got out of the hospital, and I did. Somewhat to my surprise, it went to the top of the pop charts in Britain—it was number two for a couple of weeks—and it won me a whole new set of fans.

But I'm getting ahead of my story. I didn't literally get back on my feet—that is, out of the wheelchair—until March. In between sessions of physical therapy, I practiced my flute with a vengeance. By January, I think it was, I was able to go back onstage, to play the same concerto with my friend Marisa Robles that we had played for the queen and Prince Philip. It was in Marisa's hometown, Madrid, and the warmth of the audience's response was unbelievable. I might add here that over the years, Marisa has played that concerto with me more than with any other flute player.

I also performed in many other venues. I played in chamber ensembles, for example, especially with my old friends the London Virtuosi. But after a while I had to stop that because I just couldn't fit in all the performances they wanted to do with the solo opportunities that were coming my way. Playing solo with an orchestra, to an audience of two or three thousand, took priority over doing a concert with the London Virtuosi, which at that time was playing mostly in smaller venues, the under-five-hundred halls. Although the whole thing is not about money, it's nice if you do get paid.

Another important aspect of my solo venture was making TV appearances. Things have changed since then, but there was a lot of classical music on TV in those days, and very popular it was, too. While I was still in the wheelchair, I was asked to do a program for the BBC's *World of Music* series. I quickly discovered the enormous reach of television. Suddenly, I became a sort of popular icon, recognized not only in the music world but also by the public, in airports and on the street. I remember one day I went to Selfridge's in

London to buy some tea and biscuits. A lady looked at me and said, "Don't you have a secretary who can do this for you?" I thought to myself, I've only just started on TV, and she must think I'm already a millionaire!

I also appeared on shows like Val Doonican's. Val was an Irishman who had a show on the BBC, in which he sat in a rocking chair in front of a fireplace and sang songs and played his guitar. He had me on as a guest to play "Annie's Song," and this prompted another jump in sales of the record.

I soon became fairly notorious. I even got my own show and had guests like Jessye Norman and Kyung-Wha Chung and the fine young black conductor Calvin Simmons. Sadly, Calvin died not long afterward, in a freak canoeing accident. I even had my brother, George, on the show once, playing his clarinet, which he does superbly. At one point we did Vivaldi's *The Four Seasons*, with the Zagreb Soloist Ensemble. "Spring" was a scream—we had everyone sitting in windows playing away, with window boxes full of flowers. It was very funny to watch.

Then we played *The Four Seasons* in the Albert Hall. It was rather a great event anyway, with the hall absolutely jam-packed, but two things happened to make it even more special. The first was that Ian Anderson, the founder and leader of the rock group Jethro Tull, came to the concert. I think Ian might be the only person in the world to play the flute in a major rock band. Ian came backstage before the concert and saw that I was having trouble moving about, so he lent me his walking-stick flute, and I used that to hobble on and off the stage. To the delight of the sudience, I played an encore on the walking stick.

Second, we had arranged for Shelly Gold, who was the managing director of ICM Artists in New York, to come to London for the concert. Now, to get Shelly to do this, we had to pay his fare over and back, and that was a big deal. We were taking a real chance, because the agreement was that if he didn't like my performance, he didn't have to represent me, even though we had paid his travel expenses. But he loved it and said he would take over my American management immediately and would organize all of my concerts in the United States. That was another major turning point for me, because I do think that in order to have a successful career as a soloist, you really need to cultivate an international audience. You need to work worldwide.

I've certainly done that, traveling all around the globe and playing types of music I never would have dreamed of playing when I was a little kid studying in Belfast. For example, on a trip to Japan in 1979, I made my first Japanese record, a crossover album, conducted by my old friend Hiroyuki Iwaki. At one point I did a flute-and-guitar recital tour with Kazuhito Yamashita, and we appeared on TV with that. It was a wonderful experience. In the tour, Kazuhito played the slow movement of the *New World* Symphony by Dvořák arranged for solo guitar. He is one of the greatest musicians I have ever played with.

These were some of the highlights of my first years as a soloist, and you could say that together they formed the turning point of the career that I have enjoyed for most of my life.

6

THE SOLOIST'S
WORLD

L IFE AS A SOLOIST IS VERY DIFFERENT FROM LIFE IN an orchestra, in some ways that I had expected and in others that I hadn't. The most obvious difference is that you're trading security for freedom—and when the security is that of the best job in Europe, if not the world, that's no small thing you're giving up. Another difference is your social life. In an orchestra, you tend to make friends with the players who sit near you, which in my case meant the other flutists and the oboists. These were the musicians who sat to my left in the orchestra, such as Derek Wickens, whom I played with for years in England, and Lothar Koch, who was the first oboe in the Berlin Philharmonic. Even when you're on tour, you see these people every day. But once you're a soloist, it's completely different. As you tour around, you're lucky if you see the same person twice in a year.

The social aspect of touring can also be hard work. When I first left the Berlin Philharmonic and was trying to establish myself, I had to do a lot of early getting up and late going to bed. People wanted to see me after the concert for dinner and all that—and they still do. It put a real strain on me at first, but gradually I learned how to handle it. As time went on, I got to know people in various towns, and I would stay with them. Eventually, I made enough money to actually stay in hotels and invite my friends to meet me there for breakfast or tea or dinner.

Touring nowadays is both harder and easier. Harder, because after 9/11, security is so much more rigorous. In the old days, you just walked into the airport with all your gear, and that was it. Now it's a real nuisance with the X-rays and taking your shoes off and the rest of it. Of course, you get used to it, and you get the business of going through security down to a minimum.

On the plus side, one of my greatest delights now is that I always tour with my wife, Jeanne, and we spend every day on tour together. We have breakfast, lunch, tea, and dinner together; we walk around, visit shops, and do silly things like go on a tram and get the history of the tram from the driver. We did this in Dallas one day. We were the only people on the tram, and it was highly entertaining.

Of course, going out on your own doesn't mean that you're all alone. Throughout my life, I've been blessed to have wonderful people helping me along the way, and this was especially important once I ventured out as a soloist.

To start with, a flute soloist, like a violinist or a singer, needs an accompanist, and finding the right one is essential. Early on, I did a few concerts with Anthony Goldstone. Tony is a fine musician and first rate technically, but after playing together a few times, we found that it didn't really work because we had different ideas about music. This was especially true of encores, where I wanted to play things like "Annie's Song" and "Danny Boy" and "The Flight of the Bumblebee." I was always much more of a free spirit in the classical-music world, and Tony felt that playing "The Flight of

Sharing a quiet moment with Jeanne backstage. We're always together when on tour.

the Bumblebee" was not serious enough for him. Phillip Moll, on the other hand, who helped me prepare for my first solo record- ing, has always enjoyed playing "The Flight of the Bumblebee" and all the other showy pieces that we've done. Phillip and I have never played together exclusively—I've had many other accompanists, and Phillip has had a brilliant career as a vocal and instrumental coach, along with accompanying some very famous singers, such as Jessye Norman. Yet working with Phillip is still very special. He's almost like my brother. He knows when I'm going to breathe, and if I breathed in one spot in 1992 and changed it in 2004, he writes it all into the part, but he also reminds me that in 1992 I took a breath there.

That first recording, *Showpieces*, was the beginning of a great couple of years with RCA. We recorded it at Kingsway Hall, a mecca for classical musicians. If you recorded in London, you did it at Kingsway Hall if you possibly could. It had tremendous acoustics, and Decca and many of the other major recording companies used it for big orchestral works and for operas. Even after EMI built its Abbey Road studio back in the thirties, it used Kingsway Hall for big projects. For example, EMI recorded Furtwängler there doing *Tristan und Isolde*. I remember when I was with the Royal Philharmonic playing a Rachmaninoff piano concerto with Earl Wild and Jascha Horenstein. When I was with the London Symphony, we did the Tchaikovsky Violin Concerto with Itzhak Perlman and Alfred Wallenstein. This was the caliber of people you'd be recording with there.

I had done all of that before I joined the Berlin Philharmonic, of course, and when I came back to Kingsway Hall as a soloist, it was like coming home. It was fantastic there; you'd see the van of the London Symphony Orchestra parked outside, near the van of the Philharmonia Orchestra, and one would be pulling out and the other moving in, with the LSO recording in the afternoon and the Philharmonia in the evening. This went on nonstop. So for me to do my first two recordings there as a soloist was pretty big-time.

Chuck Gerhardt was the producer of these records, and he also conducted *Showpieces*. That record was a lot of fun to make. I've mentioned Paganini's "Moto Perpetuo"; we also did "The Flight of the Bumblebee," Chopin's "Minute Waltz," Glück's "Dance of the Blessed Spirits," and half a dozen other pieces. The recording engineer—his full name was Kenneth Wilkinson, but everybody simply called him Wilkie—had a world-class reputation. He'd done hundreds of records with Chuck, very successful records. But Wilkie recorded the flute as if it was only one instrument in an orchestra. I said, "Wilkie, we're not doing this anymore. The flute has got to stand out, like a real solo instrument. We have to have a different balance on the flute." I believe this insistence of mine started off a new way of recording solo flute.

You know, producers and sound engineers often have their own ideas about how a musician should sound. On another occasion, I was trying to record the Bach sonatas with the London Virtuosi. The producer was not getting the sort of sound I wanted. When I told him as much, he said, "Oh, but you know, you're playing Bach."

I said, "I know. But when Fischer-Dieskau sings Bach, he sounds like Fischer-Dieskau. And when he sings Wagner he still sounds like Fischer-Dieskau. I want to sound like me." Unlike Wilkie, that other chap never got the point, and I had to kill the project.

In any case, Chuck Gerhardt was an American whom RCA had sent to England many years earlier to produce its classical recordings. Before that, when he still lived in New York, his most important job was keeping Toscanini happy with RCA. He must have done it pretty well, because it was Toscanini who persuaded Chuck to study conducting. I had worked with Chuck before, making records for *Reader's Digest* of bits and pieces of classical music—things like the *Romeo and Juliet* overture. Chuck did this very well. We made *Showpieces* in only two days—of course, I had done a lot of work preparing for it back in Berlin, with Phillip Moll. Then Martha

Argerich and I had two sessions on our flute-and-piano concertos, so this was a pretty hectic and concentrated week for me.

As busy as we were, this is when I first really got to know Chuck Gerhardt, because we would go out to lunch together between sessions. Back when I played in the orchestra as a session musician, the administration didn't generally take me out to lunch. But it was different now.

I got to know some of the other RCA people pretty well, too. There was Ralph Mace, with whom I had signed the contract, and Madeleine Kasket, the lady in charge of public relations. Madeleine was a terrific PR person, and she did a lot to promote all the people who were on the label.

Then there was Robert Walker, an extraordinary man. I forget what his title was, but he was in advertising or something like that. He was so knowledgeable—every time I met him, he told me some interesting fact or another. Eventually, I realized that he had a little book with all these facts in it. Nevertheless, he was a very bright fellow. He came up with the idea of putting an advertisement in *Gramophone* magazine that consisted of this simple question: "What's an Irishman doing playing the flute in Berlin?" That's all it said. The following month, RCA took out another ad announcing the two records that I'd made.

Both of them received Gold Record awards, and the one with Martha is now an icon among flute records. After seeing how successful these albums were, RCA signed me to another contract to do several more.

That second deal with RCA reminds me of how much the recording industry has changed since then. The contract involved doing three classical recordings and one crossover. Nowadays, the proportion is usually one classical to ten crossovers, if you're lucky. In those days, plenty of money was available for these productions. Today, if I wanted to make a recording with an orchestra or a large group, it would be almost impossible to get a record company to pay for it.

It was in the course of that second contract that Ralph Mace became my producer. I was making an album with a bunch of pieces, including "Annie's Song," with Chuck Gerhardt as producer and conductor. We were doing some of them at Kingsway Hall, but we went to Walthamstow Town Hall for some of them. It was during one of those sessions that I had a really bad argument with Chuck in front of the orchestra. I don't remember what had set Chuck off, but he was being abusive to me, and I wasn't going to take it. I noticed that the green light was on, and this meant the whole conversation was being recorded. I asked Chuck to come into the control room, and I had the technician play back the conversation. Well, Chuck was very embarrassed, but it was too late. His behavior had ended our relationship as artist and producer.

This is where Ralph Mace came in. Ralph had never done anything like producing a record, but I believed he could do it. Our first recording took place in RCA's Whitfield Street studios, and it was in these studios that we met Mike Ross. Mike was the recording engineer, and he and Ralph hit it off right away. Ralph knew the sound he was after, and Mike knew how to help him get it. Ralph became a very close friend, and we recorded many things together, including the world premiere of Joaquín Rodrigo's *Concierto pastoral*, John Corigliano's *Pied Piper Fantasy*, and the concertos of Saverio Mercadante.

I always enjoyed going to RCA's offices, which were on Curzon Street in Mayfair. That part of London is very fancy. Every time I went there, I passed a dealership that sold Rolls-Royces and Bentleys, and even though I don't drive, I thought, Oh, man, one day I'd like to get a Rolls-Royce. I nearly did, but then I bought a Bentley instead.

I had many wonderful colleagues in those days. One of the most important to me was a man named David Overton. You may never have heard of him, since he often works behind the scenes. He was a chorister at Westminster Abbey and had also gotten into composition and arranging—he did many arrangements for a group called the King's Singers. He arranged the music for two of my recordings, the Christmas ones. He also transcribed some pieces for me that were originally written for another instrument. The first one was Rodrigo's *Fantasia para un gentilhombre*, written for the guitar. Most recently, I had an unusual assignment for him. We were preparing for a flute conference in New York this summer—that is, August 2009—which would include a huge extravaganza with hundreds of flutes playing together. We needed a special piece for the occasion, so I asked David to do a medley of some favorite tunes and then arrange it for four-part harmony. I'm very pleased with what he came up with, which we've called the "Galway Fantaisie."

David and I have had a lot of fun times together. I wanted to do something special for his fiftieth birthday, and I decided to take him to Italy. He lives in Grimsby, in the north of England, and to make the schedule work out, I had to pick him up there in a private jet to fly to London. Then we changed to a commercial airliner for the flight to Venice and went on from there to Padua.

In one sense the trip was wasted on David. He's a very conservative English type of eater—prawn cocktail, steak and chips, that kind of thing. Whereas I was experimenting with all these terrific Italian dishes, everything I could get onto my plate. But it didn't matter—he loved it, and we had a great time.

At one point I recorded the Mozart concertos with the New Irish Chamber Orchestra at Maynooth College, near Dublin. That recording was awarded the Grand Prix du Disque. The conductor was André Prieur, who was one of the leading musicians in Ireland. Once when I was touring in the United States, I had to take a private plane from Boston to New York. There were some extra seats, so I took the senior members of the orchestra with me, including André. He sat with the pilot and was so enamored of the whole experience that he began to take flying lessons and got his pilot's

Wherever you are, there's always time for a little fun. The egg and I—as captured by Akira Kinoshita, the famous Japanese photographer, in 1994—is one of my favorite pictures.

license. I never flew with him, but some of my friends did and said he was very good. I loved him as a friend and a colleague. He was an excellent conductor and a very fine flute player.

Another person who had a big influence on me and became a close friend was Henry Mancini. He was also a flute player, and we both had flutes made by Mr. Cooper. The two of us got on like a house on fire.

Henry and I first met sometime in the early eighties. We wanted to make a recording together, so we arranged a meeting in London to plan it. We booked a room in a Georgian house that rented space for use as studios, somewhere near Hyde Park Corner. Inside the room was a beautiful grand piano and nothing else. When Henry and I showed up at this house, he had the charts already written for some of his songs, which he had arranged for flute. I have to confess that I didn't know half of the pieces he brought, but I did appreciate who was playing the piano for me. I knew that he was a giant in the music business and had all these great films under his belt, especially *The Pink Panther.*

You might say that Henry wrote the background music for America, the way Verdi wrote the background music for Italy. In fact, there are probably more people alive today who know Henry Mancini's "Pink Panther" than know the march from *Aïda.*

We got down to business, and Henry produced his charts. I sight-read my way through them, and we discussed how we were going to proceed, changing the keys as needed. Then Henry went away and rearranged the pieces as we had decided. He sent me the new charts, I learned them all, and we went to a studio and recorded them. In the studio, Henry was extremely funny. His language was always full of the Anglo-Saxon picturesque. Once he even gave me lessons in how to swear, but I can't reproduce any of that in this book.

We recorded a bunch of his tunes, like "The Pink Panther," "The Molly Maguires," and the "Pennywhistle Jig." I actually introduced Henry to the pennywhistle. He used to play the "Pennywhistle Jig" on the piccolo, and I played it on the pennywhistle—the tin whistle. We played it in the key of D, and it suited the tin whistle perfectly. At one point I told him, "Listen, Henry, when you write something for the tin whistle, write it in D or G, or in E minor or B minor." So, what does he do? He arranges the "Baby Elephant Walk" with a bunch of A flats and C naturals in it. Not at all convenient for your average tin-whistle player.

Speaking of the tin whistle, somewhere along the line the press got hold of the story the wrong way around. One journalist wrote that I started on the tin whistle, and others picked that up. It sounds very romantic, going from the tin whistle to an international career on the flute. In fact, I learned the flute first, and then at some point I got a tin whistle, which uses the same sort of fingering. However, I never really learned to play it properly. In Belfast when I was a boy, the type of Irish folk music that's played on the tin whistle was the sole property of the Catholic population, so I never got into it. But I had always kept a tin whistle around, and it was fun now to play it in public with Henry.

We knew what we were trying to achieve with these recordings. Music is an international thing, for everyone to listen to and enjoy. I believe we should be involved, as musicians, with bringing music to as many people as possible. This is what we were trying to do with these crossover recordings. Ralph Mace and others at RCA were aiming to reach a wider audience, and they thought they could do this with me playing Henry Mancini's music on the flute. I have to say, we sold a ton of records.

We did some of the recording in Whitfield Street. Ralph was my producer, as usual, and Mike Ross was the technical guy. Of course, recording in a studio in Whitfield Street is very different from recording in Kingsway Hall—a very different atmosphere. ·

I had great fun fooling around with Hank Mancini on more than one occa-
sion. Here are three such times captured by the camera.

In the course of these sessions, I learned that there were managers and publicity people and agents in the listening room, all doing deals while we were trying to record. Ralph told me about this, and I went in there and said to them all, "There's no one allowed in the studio while I'm recording." They thought I was a bit weird, throwing my weight around, but if they wanted to have a business meeting, there were plenty of other rooms in Whitfield Street where they could do it. They didn't need to be entertained by me record-ing while they talked.

I've mentioned Madeleine Kasket, the PR lady for RCA. She always did a wonderful job. She considered it to be one of her duties to bring together various people in the music world. As a result, we often had quite nice lunches. I wouldn't say they were lavish, but we went to good restaurants and met some fascinating people. One day Madeleine and I had lunch with Sherrill Milnes. This was a highlight of my life. I admired this man so much, especially for his *Rigoletto* with Pavarotti and Joan Sutherland. This is probably my very favorite recording of any opera of all time, because all three of them sing so magnificently on it.

But my absolute favorite person at these recording sessions was Dolly Williamson, the lady in charge of ensuring that the sessions ran well. She would order food in for the whole crew: piles of sushi, masses of sandwiches, gallons of coffee. By the time we finished a recording, I might have put on ten pounds, because every time I went into the listening room, all this food was lying around, and I would just pick something up and eat it.

In the sessions themselves, we were under considerable pressure, because everything had to be perfect—the intonation, the interpre-tation, everything. Sadly, a lot of musicians think that simply playing the notes is enough, and they leave it at that. But all music has a hid-den depth that you have to bring out, no matter what you're playing. All music has a spirit, and whether it's a spirit of happiness, a spirit of sadness, or a spirit of longing for something, you have to reach in and capture that spirit. I think this is one of the qualities Henry enjoyed about my playing—the fact that I really got into it.

Meanwhile, my record with Henry was so successful that we organized a summer tour. We traveled all over the United States playing Henry's music, and this was a lot of fun. In the first half of each performance he played the piano, and then in the second half we played music from the record, including the "Pennywhistle Jig" and his famous version of "76 Trombones." Henry had arranged "76 Trombones" for two flutes, and it began with him playing second flute, going *do-dl-ee do-dl-ee do-dl-ee do-dl-ee* for two bars before I came in. But when we did it at "A Capitol Fourth"—the annual Fourth of July celebration on the Mall in Washington, D.C.—I let him play about sixteen bars before I came in. He got a special round of applause for playing *do-dl-ee do-dl-ee do-dl-ee do-dl-ee* over and over again.

Funny things happened along the way. During the tour, I met a girl who was trying to become Miss Wisconsin or something like that. This was the first time I'd met anyone who was in the running to be a beauty queen. Part of the competition was a talent show. This girl played the flute, and she wanted to play the *Carmen* Variations. I said, "Look, do me a favor. Choose something simple, because you're going to get there, and you may get a music director who can't read a score, and who's not used to that sort of thing, and he'll get all the tempos wrong, and you'll have a really hard time doing this." But she was determined to play the Bizet, and off she went. She later wrote to me to tell me that I had been right—everything I had told her would happen did happen, and if she had taken my advice she might have won the contest.

During this period, I got to know Henry and his wife, Ginny, very well. When Jeanne and I got married, they gave us a special party at their home in Beverly Hills. In one room Henry had a little bar, and behind it were about two dozen Grammy trophies. It was only then that I realized *exactly* how famous Henry was.

I remember the first time I visited his studio. Above the door hung a black-and-white painting. The background was black, and there were five white lines—the lines of the staff—with three white notes on them. They were the first three notes of "Moon River." Someone had painted this for Henry and had given it to him. When I came into the room and looked at it, he said, "You know, those three notes paid for my kids' education."

Henry Mancini and Johnny Mercer wrote "Moon River" for Audrey Hepburn to sing in *Breakfast at Tiffany's*, and it won both an Academy Award and a Grammy. This tune illustrates one of Henry's great gifts as a composer: his ability to write unforgettable melodies. But his real genius was matching the mood of the film, whatever it might be—from *The Creature from the Black Lagoon* to *Days of Wine and Roses* to *The Thorn Birds* to *The Pink Panther*. The Pink Panther really took off like blazes, because the filmmakers decided that the cartoon figure used in the opening credits of the Inspector Clouseau films could be spun off on its own. So you had all these cartoons of the Pink Panther with Henry's music. This was an enormous source of income for him, and it helped make his music known and loved all around the world.

Henry was an old-fashioned fellow who liked to write his music down on paper. Of course, he also had all the necessary audio technology, because, as he explained to me, many, perhaps most, film producers and directors can't read music—not that you'd expect them to, after all. This meant that Henry had to make a tape of each piece so that people could listen to it and say, "Okay, that's good, we'll have that."

He was a great teacher, and Ginny helped keep that legacy alive after his death through the Henry Mancini Institute. Unfortunately, it closed down a couple of years ago, but in the course of a decade, it gave scholarships to hundreds of young musicians working toward professional careers, and it also provided music-education programs for thousands of schoolchildren in the Los Angeles area.

Henry would have loved that, because he got along so well with kids. Once when I went to stay with him, I had my three younger children with me, and Henry started to speak pidgin German to them. He would speak English with a German accent, with the odd German word thrown in. They nearly died laughing at the things he said. Another time, when I was playing at the Aspen Festival, we had Chris Mancini, Henry's young grandson, come stay with us. Chris spent two weeks palling around with my son Patrick, and he was a charming little boy.

I often took my kids to Aspen in those days—it was easy to do, because musicians who played in the festival were given the use of a house for free. Aspen was very special. Jorge Mester was the general music director and conducted the main orchestra. Aspen is where I met the conductor Peter Bay for the first time, playing John Corigliano's *Pied Piper*. Peter and I became lifelong friends. Recently, Jeanne and I played with his orchestra in Austin, Texas, and it was fantastic to see him again.

John Denver came to one of the concerts, and we played "Annie's Song" together for the audience and made a video of it. We also did a concert with the Chieftains in Aspen, and you can't imagine what that was like. My son Patrick made a big impression. He had a rubber imitation of—I'm not sure how to put it—dog leavings, shall we say, which he carried with him everywhere and placed near people's feet when they weren't looking. One time at Wolf Trap, a guy came with a bucket and a shovel to clean it up. Finally, someone threw it away, and Patrick had a fit.

At some point I bought Patrick a fake hand—he was into magic at the time. One of the tunes the Chieftains performed at Aspen was "Give Me Your Hand." As an introduction, Paddy Maloney would make a speech about the great seventeenth-century Irish harpist O'Carolan. Harpists in those days traveled about, staying in the great houses and entertaining their hosts. Paddy told the story of how the lady of the house on one of these estates insulted the blind harpist,

Hoisting a flute of champagne and sharing a bit of conversation with John Denver at his wedding to Cassie Delaney in 1988.

Joking around with the Chieftains.

and he left in a huff. She went after him, saying, "Give me your hand! Give me your hand!" I had decided that I would give Paddy Maloney the fake hand, but I forgot to bring it onstage with me. So, during one number, I said to Paddy, "Listen, I have to leave the stage for a minute—I need to use the men's room." That was acceptable there—it wasn't the most formal concert. So I slipped out and got the hand, and when Paddy launched into his "Give me your hand" story, I took out the hand and gave it to him. Everyone cracked up, including his nibs, Paddy.

I believe the Capitol Fourth concert where Henry and I did "76 Trombones" is the only one he and I did together, but in all I played at three or four. There were lots of memorable moments. One time the great blind singer and pianist Ray Charles came on and did "Georgia," and the whole place just exploded. Another time the conductor was Rostropovich. I think he didn't have a knack for doing outdoor concerts, because in the middle of the performance he turned around and began conducting the audience while the orchestra fell to pieces. I called out to him, "Hey, Slava! Conduct the orchestra, for heaven's sake.

I appeared at a Capitol Fourth with Erich Kunzel, and it was just great. During the rehearsal, someone had the idea of having me play "Stars and Stripes Forever" on the piccolo. I said, "Okay." I thought I was going to stand in the orchestra and take cover with the other piccolo players, but no, they had me on a ramp way downstage, on my own. Naturally, I didn't have a piccolo with me, so I had to borrow one from another player. Then I had trouble remembering how the tune went, but my memory kicked in just in time.

At some point, a fan had sent me a fancy scarf, with stars and stripes like the American flag, and I wanted to wear it as a cravat. My British management said, "Oh, no—you're not supposed to wear an American flag." But it wasn't a real flag, only a scarf using the motif of the flag, so I did wear it, and it was a big hit.

At one Capitol Fourth we wanted to perform a piece from that great Irish show *Riverdance*. We got a whole troupe of young dancers ready to do it, but at the very last minute, we learned that we couldn't get permission from Michael Flatley's management, which was a terrible disappointment for the dancers. So what we did was, we played the music, and the kids danced offstage. The cameras panned around the audience and eventually panned onto the dancers.

Any time I played in these Fourth of July celebrations, there were millions of people with Irish flags, green scarves, and other Irish paraphernalia, all standing and cheering. It didn't matter a scrap to them that I came from Belfast and not from Dublin or Cork or, well, Galway.

7

PUBLIC LIFE,
PRIVATE LIFE

NINETEEN SEVENTY-EIGHT WAS A WONDERFUL year for me. It was the year my career took off in America, and it was the year I met Jeanne.

My career took off in the States because Shelly Gold was as good as his word. He had said he would take over my U.S. management, and he did a terrific job. I had a few concerts in the Hollywood Bowl that had already been planned by Ernest Fleischmann, and then I came to New York to play with the Mostly Mozart festival. It was amazing to walk along Columbus Avenue next to Lincoln Center and see a whole row of posters advertising the concert. They already had banners pasted over them: SOLD OUT. I wish I'd taken a picture of that. Both the Mostly Mozart and the Hollywood Bowl concerts were runaway successes. We had standing ovations at each one, and it seemed my career was assured in the United States.

After Mostly Mozart, I went up to Brewster, about fifty miles north of New York City, to meet my friend Julius Baker, the solo flutist of the New York Philharmonic. He was giving a master class there. I got to meet Hubert Laws and listen to him play; he was a wonderful flutist. Gary Shocker, a young flutist at the time, was also there. Now he's a well-established composer, as well as a very accomplished flute player. And among the other flute players there was a young lady named Jeanne Cinnante.

Jeanne was hanging out with a clique of girls, and she came over to me and said, "How would you like to come and have a drink with us tonight?"

I thought, Well, there's not much else happening in Brewster; I'll go for it.

So these kids came and picked me up at Julie Baker's house, where I was staying, and we drove to a bar. We looked at the menu, and hamburgers were the most interesting item on it. I was amazed, however, at the variety of drinks one could order in a little bar like this in a small town way out in the country. I decided, I'm going to try some of these drinks that have colors in their name—Blue Lagoon, White Russian, Black Velvet, and many others whose names escape me. Jeanne was the most amusing of the girls, and I was attracted by her good humor and her deep interest in the flute.

After I had had a few of these colored drinks and a hamburger, it got to be time to return to Julie's house. The girls drove me back, and I said good-bye to them and opened the front door. Julie had two Doberman pinschers, Heidi and Max. They greeted me with snarls and growls, and I tell you, these dogs were smelling me as if I were instant food. I managed to get to my room without being mauled, and I was never so happy in my life to close a bedroom door. I could hear these two suspicious beasts discussing me outside the door for quite some minutes before I fell asleep.

The following day, my friend Robert White, the tenor, came up to Brewster. At Julie's invitation he sang a few songs, and I played the flute with him for the class. Afterward, Robert's brother Philip drove us all back to New York through the pouring rain. He gave Jeanne a ride, too—she lived right around the corner from his apartment, so it was all very convenient.

I kept up contact with Jeanne after that, but in a casual way, because I was married at the time. But Annie began to be fed up with my being constantly away on tour, leaving her in Lucerne with the kids. Then, after a couple of years, Annie decided to, well, change the rules, so I decided the rules would change for me, too.

One day I was back in New York, at Carnegie Hall, preparing to play a recital. I went to the little office to talk to Rudy Stewart, the house manager, and there was Jeanne. It turned out that she was doing a rehearsal that morning. She was just chatting away with Rudy, and I asked her, "What are you doing for lunch tomorrow?"

"Nothing," she said.

And I said, "Okay, let's have lunch together."

We settled on a restaurant, Fiorello's on Broadway, across from Lincoln Center, and the next day I went there with Philip White. Jeanne turned up with a friend of hers, because she didn't trust me an inch, or so she told me later. Anyway, we all had lunch, and that started something, because after that day, whenever I was in New York, we always met for lunch or dinner.

Finally, I realized that I had a serious decision to make. Annie and I had split up, and I had become pretty serious about Jeanne. But she might not be in New York much longer. Her career was doing rather well, and I could see that she was just about to get a job as first flute in one of the provincial orchestras, and I thought, I don't want to carry on a relationship like that.

The situation came to a head one day when I was walking around Amsterdam. It was a rainy day, and I could feel the sadness in the atmosphere. Everybody looked so down in the mouth, even though they were walking by all these wonderful buildings, like the Rijksmuseum—it's really a beautiful building, which houses one of the great collections of Dutch art.

My thoughts strayed to the good times I had spent in New York with Jeanne, so I called her up and asked her if she'd like to come to Europe. After thinking about it for a while, she said she would. We fixed up a time and arranged that Jeanne would meet me in Munich while I was on tour in Germany. I was playing the night before at Neustadt, and returning to Munich meant getting up at five in the morning and changing trains twice. Changing trains should not have been difficult, because Phillip Moll was with me, and he knew the timetables of German trains almost from memory. However, we made the mistake of asking a German railway employee which train went to Munich, and we boarded the train he indicated. A few seconds before it departed, Phillip had a bad feeling, and sure enough, we were on the wrong train. We jumped off just in time to catch the correct train, which got us to Munich for breakfast.

Upon arrival in Munich, we went to the little hotel where I was staying, the Hotel an der Oper, around the corner from the opera house. At the front desk, the clerk informed me that my wife was upstairs sleeping. Well, *that* was interesting.

I went straight upstairs, and there was Jeanne in bed. She later told me that she had bought a new nightgown for the occasion. I said to her, "Jeannie, come on! You've got to get out of bed—we need to have breakfast, quick!" It was already quite late—nearly ten o'clock.

She got dressed, and we went to a restaurant that served sausages and beer—a typical Bavarian breakfast. Jeanne had never seen anything like this, especially at ten thirty in the morning—Phillip digging into a pig's foot, and waitresses carrying four and five steins of beer, just like in the movies. We ordered a plate of assorted sausages, and this was Jeanne's first and last breakfast of this type.

We spent the rest of the day together in Munich and then gradually made our way to Switzerland, passing through a few other little places like Salzburg. I had booked a room at the Goldener Hirsch, a charming and romantic hotel that just happens to be on the street where Mozart lived, Getreidegasse. We arrived in the evening, and Jeanne wanted to get her passport stamped at the station. We had already come through immigration, but as it turned out we were right near the Austrian Railway Police station. I told her, "Hold on a minute." I went into the police station and said, "Listen—can you do me a favor and stamp this passport for my American girlfriend?

She's into all that stuff." So with good humor they stamped it: "Bundespolizei, Station Sieben und Dreissig, Salzburg"—Federal Police, Station 37, Salzburg.

Jeanne was happy with that, and we proceeded to have a nice dinner by candlelight in our hotel room. The next morning we set out down Getreidegasse, which was wall-to-wall people. It looked as if the entire population of Asia was visiting. As we walked along, I stopped in front of Mozart's house, but Jeanne didn't know that's what it was. There's a little grocer's shop on the ground floor, and she was marveling at the display of Austrian specialties in the window. "Look at all this lovely stuff!" she exclaimed. The items displayed in the window were so different from those she was used to in the States.

I said, "Hey, did you know Mozart was born on the first floor up there?"

She took a step back into the crowd and cried out, "Wow!" three times. Everyone moved back, as if they thought she was going to give a political speech.

I rescued her from being the center of attention and led her upstairs. On the way, I pointed out where Mozart used to play football in the yard behind the house, and I showed her Mozart's piano and the picture of his father, a lock of his hair, and the little stove where Mrs. Mozart used to burn the breakfast. That was our first visit together to Salzburg. Needless to say, Jeanne photographed the whole place from top to bottom.

Then we headed to Switzerland on the train and eventually arrived in Lucerne. Jeanne was amazed by my apartment because it was so clean and neat—she couldn't believe that I lived there on my own. In fact, I had a wonderful cleaning lady, and she kept the place spotless. She always did an especially good job the day before I was due to come back from a tour. I showed Jeanne around Lucerne and introduced her to my kids. She loved them, they loved her, and she spoiled them to death. That was the beginning of our courtship.

Meanwhile, I had a U.S. tour scheduled, and Jeanne came with me. It was during this tour, in Victoria, Texas, that I asked her to marry

Jeanne and me on our wedding day, September 9, 1984, in Vitznau, Switzerland. It was sheer bliss.

me. I said, "Listen, you have to think about this for a couple of weeks. Don't tell anybody, but just think about it. You've seen how I live. You know what the score is. And I don't want any more kids. I think if you want to get married on those terms, we could do it. But you really have to think about what you're doing."

Well, she went for it, and we had a wonderful wedding in Switzerland, at the Park Hotel in Vitznau. We have very fond memories of that day—not least, of the many friends who were there. Sadly, that was the last time I would see Shelly Gold, who had been so instrumental in getting my career up and running in America. He died suddenly just a few months later.

Our wedding was in 1984. And the rest, as they say, is history.

Of course, there were some logistical details to deal with, and certain aspects of my life that Jeanne had to adjust to. I was already rather famous. I tried up to a point to ignore this fame and lead a normal life. I tried to be with Jeanne simply as a normal guy and not make a big deal of the fact that I was playing with the Philharmonic this week and the Symphonic the next week and the Othermonic the week after that. But it's very difficult to do both—to play it down *and* maintain a public profile. Indeed, many musicians come to feel that they don't have private lives at all.

In our case, it helped right from the start that Jeanne is a flute player herself, who understands what I do. For years now, she has played the flute with me onstage, and we both love that. In the very beginning, we didn't perform together, but she came on tour with me whenever she could, and we hung out together when I wasn't rehearsing or performing. Jeanne was my companion—my buddy, so to speak. We did everything together—we went to the movies and to restaurants, and we walked up and down streets looking in every shop window. Window-shopping is something we still enjoy to this day.

Playing together remains the most fun. Jeanne and me in London in 2007.

Very shortly after we got married, I had to go on tour. The first part of it was on a cruise ship in the Mediterranean. This was a French-run ship called the *Mermoz*, after Jean Mermoz, the first Frenchman to fly across the Atlantic. André Borocz, who ran music festivals in France, and his wife, Jackie, had sold the owners on the idea of having musical cruises, which they called the Music Festival at Sea. These were very successful, and I loved them. The cast consisted of the most popular classical musicians of the day, and we all played together in chamber-music concerts on board.

Well, this time I had to take Jeanne shopping and buy her four different gowns, because this was one of those fancy cruises where the ladies are supposed to wear a different color every evening—they have silver night, gold night, red night, and whatnot night. I remember our buying a red dress that looked like a cinema curtain. We still have all those dresses, and every time we come across the "red cinema curtain," we start laughing and recall that first cruise together.

At one point, Jeanne wanted to have her hair done, at a port we had pulled into. She had already been there on another cruise, when she and a friend had played as a flute-and-guitar duo. We found the open-air shop that she remembered, down by the beach, and the beautician did Jeanne's hair up and stuck some plastic knitting-needle-type ornaments through it. It looked great. Jeanne said, "Oh, this is a good deal, Jimmy—this doesn't cost so much at all." The next time we were in New York, we saw the same ornaments in a shop for half the price.

When we returned to Lucerne after the cruise, the first thing we had to address was our living arrangements. I had a little apartment in Haldenstrasse, no. 12. It had a large sitting room upstairs with a kitchen; the bedroom was downstairs, with two other little rooms that had originally been bedrooms. One of them was my office,

At a postconcert party in Florida in 1984, celebrating once again my marriage to Jeanne, this time with Mikhail Baryshnikov.

and I had converted the other one into a walk-in wardrobe where I could hang my clothes.

Then Jeanne arrived with all *her* possessions. At the beginning it was not so bad, but as life together progressed, we needed more space. So we rented a second apartment across the street and divided our things up between the two. The trouble with this solution was that every time we wanted something, it was in the wrong place—it was across the road, or if we were across the road, it was back at no. 12.

So we decided to look for a house. It took us ages, because in all the houses we saw, in the price range we were looking at, the bedrooms were so small that you couldn't swing a cat in them. Not that bedroom cat-swinging is high up on my list of amusements, but there was truly just enough room for a bed, and you could have touched the walls when you were lying in it.

Then a friend who lived nearby told us to go and look at a house in Meggen, a romantic little village along Lake Lucerne, or the Vierwaldstättersee, to give it its Swiss-German name.

At the time, I thought Meggen was a place where only rich people lived, and I decided against even going to look at the house. Then I had a talk with George Bauer, the friend who had told us about it in the first place, and he said, "Look, I know this house is bigger than you want. But what you do is, you move into it and close off a few rooms. Then if you need more space, you open up the rooms."

So we arranged to see the house, and the trip from Lucerne to Meggen was a real scream. We drove there in two cars; I rode with the gentleman who owned the house, Dr. Edward Gubelin, and Jeanne rode with Walter Nüssli, who looked after my business affairs in Switzerland. Walter was driving his old Rolls-Royce, and Dr. Edward Gubelin had a two-tone Mercedes. As you may know, they don't make two-tone Mercedeses—he had to have it specially painted. It was the color of tigereye, light brown and dark brown, and he had taken the Mercedes symbol off the front and put a big ball of tigereye in its place. When we got into the car, he retrieved a pair

In our beautiful garden in Meggen. I loved it from the very first moment I saw it.

In the garden again, in January 2009, with two friends from the Israel Camerata: on my right, the music director, Avner Biron, and on Jeanne's left, the general manager, Ben Shira. But what I really want you to notice are the mountains that we look at every day when we are at home.

of white gloves from the glove compartment and pulled them on. As we drove along, we discussed this, that, and the other thing, but not the price of the house. At some point he said, "You know, when I was a boy, we always had these klaxon horns, but you're not allowed to have them now in Switzerland." Then he put his hand under the dashboard and squeezed something, and the old klaxon went off. He had had one built into his car on the quiet.

After twenty minutes or so, we arrived at the house, and Dr. Gubelin said, "Why don't you have a walk around the garden while I undo the security?" The security that he had for this house was a rather old-fashioned system involving window shutters and various electrical devices. So I walked around with Walter and Jeanne in the most beautiful garden I had ever seen—it was like the Garden of Eden, with a view to the south looking over Lake Lucerne and the Alps. It was a clear, sunny day, and I said, "Jeannie, I don't care what this house looks like inside—we've got to buy it just to sit in the garden." It was at this point that Walter said we should buy the house and then burn it down and build another with the insurance money. I did not follow this piece of advice.

Then Dr. Gubelin called us, and we went inside and started looking around. The house wasn't in very good condition. Dr. Gubelin hadn't lived there for two years, and for ten years before that his wife had been in a wheelchair, and they had inhabited only the ground floor. But I could see that it had been a fine house and that it had real possibilities.

That evening, I told Jeanne, "Listen, tomorrow I'm going to get up early and go along and see Dr. Gubelin, and we'll try to buy this house. He told me how much he wanted for it, and I think I can manage it." His asking price was three and a half million Swiss francs (not quite two million U.S. dollars at the time), which for a house and garden that large was a very good deal.

The next day I had breakfast with Dr. Gubelin and Walter Nüssli. Dr. Gubelin said, "Well, this is the price of the house, and that's it. This is what I need to live on, so I don't think I'm going to go down."

"Okay," I said. "I would like to buy this house."

Then Walter asked, "Shall I make a *Vorvertrag*?" (That's a kind of precontract.)

And I said, "No, what do you mean? If Dr. Gubelin says he's going to sell it, and I say I'm going to buy it, we'll shake hands and that's a deal."

Dr. Gubelin loved this and agreed on the spot. Back in those days in Switzerland, a jeweler would simply hand a potential buyer a bag of diamonds and say, "Choose what you want and send the rest back." This was done on a handshake. I don't know whether that way of doing business still stands, but Dr. Gubelin thought it was great.

Phillip Parker, my English accountant, helped us get a mortgage. But before the papers were in order so that we could take possession, I had to go on tour again. In fact, I went off the very day I shook hands with Dr. Gubelin.

Jeanne took charge of everything, and while I was away, she gave me daily reports. Before she closed down the apartments in Haldenstrasse, she had one bedroom of the new house painted, along with what's now the living room. It was two separate rooms in those days, but we've since had a wall pulled down and made it one big room. By the time I came back from my tour—on my birthday, December 8—she had the rooms all set up. We were ready to begin our new life in our own house, where we're living to this day.

When we first moved in, the house had about ten rooms, and we thought that was enormous. But we've recently built on another six rooms, with an elevator. I say "we," but it was actually Jeanne who took charge of this building project. She was the one who hired architects and the other contractors and got the thing built. She has really made this a wonderful home.

The new part of the house is where Esther, our secretary, has her office, and Jeanne has *her* office. There's a gymnasium, and Jeanne has her own personal room to practice in. Above all this, on the top floor, is a large bedroom, which you can definitely swing cats

Yes, that's me in the kitchen at home in Meggen, wielding the fondue pot (above), but I never go very far without my flute (right).

in, with both hands. It has windows on the south and west sides, enabling us to look out over the garden, past Lake Lucerne, to the mountains in the south. I look forward to coming home to this paradise after every tour.

We have some very special friends here. There's a well-known Swiss sculptor named Rolf Brem, and the Swiss surgeon Bruno Vogt—the man who put my legs back together after the accident thirty years ago. I have another Swiss friend, Walter Vollmeier; we go tromping up and down mountains together—and we do a fair amount of "tea" drinking together, too. Walter was my next-door neighbor on Haldenstrasse and now lives in Meggen, a little way down the lake from us. And, of course, there's Rainer Lafin. He's a good friend, as well as a trusted collaborator. He's a great flute craftsman who developed a type of head joint that I love to use. He's also the godfather to my second son, Patrick. He actually lives in Germany, but he's just over an hour away, and he frequently visits us in Meggen.

Of course, many of our friends are fellow musicians and people we've met while on tour. When we return to familiar towns, it's nice to catch up with our good old friends and see how they're progressing. Many have grown children by now, and some have, like me, become grandparents. In this business, the fact that I consider someone my friend doesn't mean I get to sit around with him all that much. I may be lucky to see someone once a year. But it's always great when I do see my friends, and I have a sense of being connected to all these people out there.

For example, Jeanne and I recently played with Peter Bay and his Austin Symphony, and we were able to arrange our schedules so as to spend about a week together. I first met Peter at Aspen nearly thirty years ago. Phillip Moll is still one of my principal accompanists, more than thirty years after we first worked together, and we enjoy a close friendship. I've played with Lorin Maazel several times this past

Posing for a bronze by my good friend, the well-known Swiss sculptor Rolf Brem.

year—in New York, London, Cardiff, and Barcelona. Lorin is one of the principal conductors in my life, going back many years, and a good friend, too. He has written two flute concertos for me.

Another of my principal conductors is Leonard Slatkin. In fact, he may even have conducted more flute concertos for me than Lorin. Leonard came into my life in the early days of his tenure as chief conductor of the St. Louis Symphony.

One learns from all good conductors, and Leonard has shown me many things, but mostly how to give. The Lucerne Symphony Orchestra had scheduled a concert for May 2010 to commemorate my seventieth birthday. This concert was not included in the normal season and was being promoted as a special event. But the orchestra was having difficulty finding a conductor. Then we learned that Leonard would be conducting around that time in Frankfurt, which is not that far from Lucerne. I got in touch with him, and he said he would be glad to do it. However, there was the question of how to find the money to pay him. He said he would do it free of charge. Well, I was very grateful, but I still felt he ought to be paid. Then one evening in London, when I was having dinner with John Corigliano, Mark Adamo, and Leonard, I again brought up the subject of remuneration. Leonard said to stop worrying about it: we had all reached the point where we could afford to do something like this for a friend. What a blessing good friends are, and what a lesson in humility that was.

I mentioned Richard Colburn in connection with my knighthood. I first met Richard on one of my early visits to Los Angeles, when I played with the Los Angeles Chamber Orchestra, and we remained very good friends until his death. Richard had been a successful businessman—I'm not sure in what business; he didn't talk much about that—but by the time I knew him, he devoted most of his time to music. He supported the Los Angeles Opera and various smaller groups. One time he had me do a concert as a fundraiser for a baroque-music group he cared about. We also did charity concerts at his house; he was a very good amateur violist, and he loved to play chamber quartets.

Richard had clearly done very well in his business career—he had houses in Beverly Hills and Palm Springs, as well as the one in Chester Square in London. But he was quite an unassuming man. When he first spoke to me of the Colburn School, I didn't take it seriously—I thought he had rented some sort of building and had a few people teaching string instruments. But that was before I visited the school. That's when I started to realize just how big Richard was. The school is a full-fledged conservatory, right across the street from Disney Hall, the famous home of the Los Angeles Philharmonic.

Mstislav "Slava" Rostropovich is another person I loved as a musician and as a friend. I've mentioned the first times I played with him, with the LSO and the Berlin Philharmonic. Fortunately, we kept meeting up again once I went out on my own.

The best times we had were on tour, especially the musical cruises on the *Mermoz*. I remember one morning I was on deck, nursing a tremendous hangover. It was about ten thirty and I was sitting there in my dressing gown and swimming trunks, trying to make up my mind whether to go for a swim. Suddenly, Slava appeared, very excited. "Jimushka!" he exclaimed. "We have to celebrate—Russian premier dead!" It turned out that Yuri Andropov had just died.

So Slava poured me out a liberal vodka from the bottle he was carrying, and we sat around talking and drinking until it was time for lunch. There were eight people at our table, and sitting next to me was a lady from L.A. who was showing a bit more of herself than one normally shows at lunch. But it was a cruise, so I didn't think too much about it.

As for Slava and me, by this time the vodka had really taken hold, and you know what they say—in vino veritas. So I was peppering him with questions: "Hey, Slava, did you play with this orchestra? What do you think about it?" And he would reply with variants on

"Jeem, thees orchestra is *sheet*." The rest of us were rolling around laughing at Slava laying into all these musical institutions.

At the end of lunch we started to get up, and Slava lurched over against this lady. I thought, Oh, man—I hope he doesn't put his hand down her dress. But he didn't. He put his hand into her handbag, and he pulled out a recording machine. He turned it off, opened it up, took out the little cassette, put it in his pocket, and gave the machine back to her.

I played with Slava many times, especially in Washington, D.C., where he was music director of the National Symphony Orchestra. I remember one piece we played was the Khachaturian violin concerto, which I had arranged for flute. Jean-Pierre Rampal had been given permission many years earlier to arrange it for flute, but he didn't—he simply played the notes as they were written for the violin. I transcribed it so that it sounded truly like a flute concerto. Slava loved it, and at his apartment after the performance he spoke of his many musician friends who were still in the Soviet Union. Sometimes he was moved to tears while speaking of them.

I loved hanging out with Slava at his apartment. He lived on his own there quite a lot, because he was based at the National Symphony, while his wife, the great soprano Galina Vishnevskaya, might be singing at the Met or Covent Garden or La Scala. Slava was not a great housekeeper. For example, if he wanted to give you a drink, you had a choice of several half-empty bottles of vodka. Between us, we demolished quite a few of those over the years.

Now, I don't want to give the impression that we were drunk out of our minds. You cannot pursue a career like the one I've had, or the one Rostropovich had, if you are drunk all the time. When you need to deliver a virtuoso performance, it is better to have a very clear head. In fact, Slava and I used to get high just from being with each other. It was a wonderful thing to know Slava, and I will never forget his playing.

. . . .

Belfast remains a very special place for me. It is a beautiful city, with all of its Georgian and Victorian architecture. But it's also a bit sad to go back there because so much has changed. My friends in Belfast became few and far between over the years, because so many of them had emigrated—to New Zealand, to Australia, to Canada. Then some government housing authority decided to go in for what they call "urban renewal" on all those little streets like Carnalea Street. They pulled down the houses that my family and our neighbors had lived in for decades and built new high-rise housing projects. Everybody seemed to be more prosperous, although I don't know how this worked, because the people in those neighborhoods weren't earning any more money than before. I guess the housing was subsidized. Meanwhile, when they tore down the old houses, the whole community disappeared.

Every now and again, when I go back to Belfast, I run into someone who says, "Jimmy, remember me? I used to live two doors down." A couple of years ago, I saw a fellow named Malcolm Beggs, who used to live next door to us, at no. 19 Carnalea Street. Malcolm told me his mother was still alive, and she was 101. I went along to visit her, and she remembered me very well. I think she's still alive today at 103. Mrs. Beggs was a seamstress, and she made clothes for us all. What I liked best was that if you brought her a piece of cloth, she would turn it into swimming trunks just like that. In fact, she made swimming trunks for all the boys on the street.

It has meant a lot to me to stay in touch with all these people I had known in Belfast, because it was a special time that we all came through together. We were all pulling the same old dead horse—what you might call financial instability. We all pulled that one together in the little streets where we lived, during the war and in the years afterward.

Sometimes these visits have taken an unexpected turn. To tell this story, I have to go back a long way, to when I was first in my uncle Joe's Onward Flute Band. One of the pieces we did was the overture to *Preciosa*, by Weber. It's a wonderful overture—Weber wrote absolutely great overtures. This particular piece is one that Uncle Joe had learned from my grandfather. It has a lot of triplet passage work in it and also a big flute solo going up to top A, which, when I was first learning the piece, was simply out of reach for me. If my dad was around when I was practicing it, he would say, "Oh, you should have heard your granddad play that—he was the only one who could play that top A." Nowadays, that doesn't sound like such a big deal. With better flutes, people play much higher. And Brazilian flute players play everything in the top octave—top A is one of their low notes.

Anyway, my dad was always telling me, "Oh, you should have heard your grandfather play this piece. He was a great player." I got a bit fed up with this.

But time rolled on, and I went away to study and eventually started my career. It was when I was with Sadler's Wells that I played my first big recital in Belfast. It was in the Hamilton Harty room at Queen's University and it went very well, and I got a big ovation. My dear old friend Havelock Nelson was playing the piano, and we were very pleased with ourselves.

Then along came this old fellow who said, "You know, I knew your granddad."

"Really?" I said.

"Yes, I knew him very well," he said.

I asked, "How did he play?"

"A bit like you," he said, "but he had better low notes."

I simply couldn't stand it.

The first time I returned to Belfast after leaving the Berlin Philharmonic was supposed to be another triumphal return for the local boy. I was going to play *The Four Seasons* with the BBC orchestra. But then my father passed away. Sadly, I did not get to see him because I arrived just after he died.

I discussed the situation with my brother, and we decided that I should go ahead and do the concert. My dad had always encouraged me in my flute playing, and he was very pragmatic—George and I could imagine him saying, "Well, dead is dead, and there's nothing you can do about it."

The wake was the next day, or maybe the day after that. Irish wakes are something else. People who never knew the deceased will look up the announcement in the newspaper and see where the wake is going to be, and then they turn up for free drinks and something to eat. That's what happened at my dad's wake. All sorts of people were there who never knew him at all. And they would say things like, "Remember me? I knew your brother, George."

I would reply, "That's George over there." Of course, they had never seen my brother before, either, unless it was from afar in a dance hall where he was playing the clarinet or the saxophone. He was more famous in Belfast than I was, as he played in several dance bands, including the famous Royal Dublin Show Band.

Then came the day of the funeral. We went to the little cemetery in Newtownards where our mother was buried, and we buried our dad right next to her. It was a sad day for us.

My old friend and fellow flute player Billy Dunwoody—who helped start off my career by putting me in touch with Muriel Dawn—was someone I always got together with when I went back to Belfast. He died very unexpectedly, from a stroke, at the age of seventy. His daughter Andrea told me that he was sitting there talking to her, and then just from one moment to the next, he fell silent. I thought, That's a great way to go, if you have to go. And, of course, we all have to go. Still, hearing that he had died was another very sad thing for me.

Billy's wife, Irene, survived him, and the next time I was in Belfast I called and asked her whether she wanted to come with me to hear the Verdi *Requiem*. Afterward, she realized that this was the first concert she'd been to since Billy died. Not only that, but it was on the anniversary of the day Jean-Pierre Rampal died. I remember thinking that it was a fitting coincidence, flutistically speaking.

Some of the shops in Belfast that I had known as a kid looked very different to me once I had started to come up in the world.

I used to go down Queen's Arcade, which has some fancy shops in it. One of them is a jewelry store owned by a gentleman named John Lunn. I bought Jeanne's engagement ring there, which was fun. She still has the ring, and we visit John Lunn's shop from time to time and spend a bit of money there.

In the old days, when I went to Billy Dunwoody's house to have a flute lesson or to practice for the trio that he and I had formed with Edmund Duke, I had to change buses in the city center. On the corner where I changed buses was a shop that sold antique silver. I used to look in the window and wonder, Who on earth would buy this stuff? What would they use it all for? I remember that they had peacocks and other birds and animals made of silver, and candlesticks, flatware, and tea services. It was all horrendously priced, I thought. But then one day when Jeanne and I were in Belfast, I said, "Jeannie, come on, I want to show you a shop where I used to look in the window when I was a kid." We went around and had a look, and lo and behold, what did we do? We bought some flatware. It's antique Irish, I think, and we use it with pride when we have special dinners.

Jeanne is a prodigious tea drinker—she drinks more tea than anyone I know. I buy her teapots now and again on festive occasions, like Easter or Christmas or her birthday, and over the years we have amassed quite a large collection. For one birthday, I went into John Lunn's, and they had a wonderful Irish teapot in silver, and I bought it. It's the most expensive teapot I've ever bought in my life—if I mentioned the price, you'd think I was completely mad. But it's beautifully crafted, and Jeanne loves it.

There's a good story connected with one of the people I always try to see when I'm in Belfast—my old friend Colin Fleming. While I was in the Berlin Philharmonic, he received a grant to come over and study with me. But he had to audition before I could take him on in the Karajan school. So he played a very difficult piece by Theobald Boehm, called "Du, du liegst mir im Herzen." Then Karajan asked him whether he could play the solo from Brahms's

Fourth Symphony, and Colin said, "Well, I don't really know it, but if you have the music, I'm sure I can play it."

Herbert ordered the music out of the orchestra's library, and, *tout de suite*, Colin played the solo, and of course he played it beautifully. So they let him come to Berlin. He studied with me for a couple of years, and then, when I left, he studied with Andreas Blau. Eventually, Colin went back to Belfast, and he has been solo flute in the Ulster Orchestra there ever since.

I especially love going to see Colin because he knows all the good restaurants—every time, we go to a different gastronomic haven, and there are plenty of them in Northern Ireland. You might be surprised to hear that, because when people in the newspapers and on television mention Belfast, all they want to talk about is the "Troubles." That kind of thing, incidentally, is one reason why reading newspapers and watching TV is something I mostly don't want to do. I prefer to read a book, play chess, or play backgammon with Jeanne—and she's a pretty good player, too.

Getting back to Belfast, though: there was one restaurant in particular that we loved, until they changed it into a sort of rowdy place—it was called Roscoff's, and for years it was voted the best restaurant in Great Britain. The food was very good at Roscoff's, and it had a wonderful wine list.

Sometimes I've encountered surprises on these visits to Ireland. At one of my concerts, I looked out at the audience and saw my cousin Ann and her mother, Sadie—Sadie was Uncle Joe's sister. I hadn't really kept up with them, but there they were at this concert, and we've stayed in touch ever since. I learned that Ann has been making a genealogical study of the family, and she has turned up quite a few new additions—mostly from the wrong side of the sheets. But it's nice to have a big family, no matter what side of the sheets they come from.

Ever since that unexpected meeting, I've tried to rearrange my schedule a bit whenever I go to Belfast. When you're on tour, all too often you arrive at the airport and grab a cab, check into the hotel, go to a rehearsal, do another rehearsal the next morning, play the concert in the evening, and then head back to the airport to fly to the next venue, where you repeat the whole cycle again. But now, when I go to Belfast, I like to see whether I can arrive a couple of days early and have time to see Ann and Sadie Black, my cousin Fred Garford, and a whole bunch of other cousins. I also like to see Billy Dunwoody's family, Irene and their two daughters, Andrea and Wilma, who are married and have families there. We get together and have a bit of a party.

We had some rough times in the old days, but Belfast was still a great place to grow up. It had a very lively musical scene, and I owe a lot to the people who helped me along the way, teaching me and encouraging me. Considering that we all had nothing, we made a lot out of it, and I don't think I'd change that for anything.

8

INSIDE THE
MUSIC

BACK WHEN MY FRIENDS IN LONDON WERE TRYING to discourage me from even thinking about a solo career, there was some truth to their argument that there are far fewer pieces written for flute than for piano or violin in the classical repertoire. One thing my friends didn't take into account, however, is that pieces written for violin or cello—or, for that matter, for voice—can easily be transcribed for the flute.

Another thing they didn't think of is that even if much of what you do is at the Bach-Mozart-Beethoven level, there is a lot of fine music from popular and traditional sources. I have always loved many different kinds of music. When my brother and I were young boys, my father introduced us to all kinds of music, from Strauss waltzes to themes of the last three great symphonies of Mozart. Dad used to play these on the accordion, which he played very well. And then we were surrounded with Irish folk music, which we heard on the radio every morning after the news, just before we went to school.

The bands I played in had a lot of very good arrangements of classical music, as well as the marches that were their stock-in-trade. We used to play a version of Mozart's *Jupiter* Symphony, and I will never forget the first time I heard the whole thing with an orchestra. It was so impressive.

As an orchestral musician, I was introduced to a huge range of music, much of which I had never even heard before. First there was the entire operatic repertoire, from Mozart to Verdi to Wagner to Britten. And then all the symphonies—Mozart and Beethoven and Brahms and Tchaikovsky and Bruckner. When I got to Berlin, we did a lot of those big Bach cantatas and masses with Karajan, and it was very inspiring to play them.

Many classical and romantic composers wrote wonderful concertos and chamber pieces featuring the flute. I've mentioned the recording of works by Prokofiev and César Franck I made with Martha Argerich. Bach, Vivaldi, and Pergolesi all wrote flute concertos that I've played many times and recorded. A special favorite of mine is the flute concerto that Jacques Ibert wrote for Marcel Moyse in the thirties, which I played most recently with Lorin Maazel, on the opening night of his final season with the New York Philharmonic. Mozart's concertos have been a staple of my career—the Concertos in D and G and the Concerto for Flute and Harp. I've played them a million times with different orchestras, and of course the first time I played for the Queen of England and the Duke of Edinburgh, it was the Concerto for Flute and Harp with Marisa Robles. The concert that Jeanne and I did recently with Peter Bay included the Mozart Concerto in D and the Cimarosa Concerto for Two Flutes.

Then there are the songs, all sorts of songs. With the Chieftains, I've played and recorded Irish songs that range from "The Battle of Deer's Leap" to "Down by the Salley Gardens," and, naturally, "Danny Boy." On trips to Japan, I've made two recordings of Japanese songs that have sold very well, and there is a little story behind this. One thing I found interesting about Japan is that at least at the less formal restaurants, if a family is there for lunch or dinner, at the end of the

With Lorin Maazel and the Pittsburgh Symphony, in the first performance of his Music for Flute and Orchestra *in 1995.*

meal, the parents would quietly sing their favorite tune with their kids. I became acquainted with a lot of good songs by listening to these families.

Once I left Berlin, I came to know personally some of the pop singers and groups whose music my buddies at Mommsenstrasse had introduced me to. The Beatles had already broken up by then, but I performed with quite a few others—Cleo Laine, Pink Floyd, Stevie Wonder, Elton John.

And of course there was "Annie's Song," which made my name known among people who would never have thought of going to a concert of classical music.

I don't regret playing any of this music, but an unintended consequence has been that people sometimes express surprise when they see me playing a concert with only classical pieces in it, such as the Mozart and Cimarosa concert in Texas with Peter Bay. Yet in fact, my training and my early professional life were completely classical, and most of the concerts Jeanne and I play are entirely or mostly classical.

Sometimes, too, people ask whether I don't get tired of playing the same music over and over—What, Mozart *again*? But if it's great music to start with, no, you don't get tired of it. An engaging newspaper reporter in Austin asked me about that, and I explained it with an analogy: "I'm thinking specifically about when you read something in the Bible. If you're reading something the first time through, you comprehend it; but then you read it again and you get more out of it; you read it a third time and you realize there's a whole lot you missed the first time. Not only that, you glimpse that there's even more connected to it that you missed before. It's the same with that Mozart concerto; the more you play it, the more you get to know what it's all about." I believe I can say that I always progress in my interpretation of the pieces I play repeatedly.

· · · · · · · ·

Discussing a fine point about our performance with my good friend Maestro Claudio Scimone.

Having said that, I will add that learning a new piece can be very exciting—especially if it's a brand-new piece that you have commissioned, and you're working out the details with the composer.

The first time I did this was near the beginning of my solo career. I had heard the guitar concerto by Joaquín Rodrigo, the great blind Spanish composer, and I loved it. I thought that if he wrote a flute concerto that sounded something like his guitar concerto, the famous *Concierto de Aranjuez*, we would be in business with an instant hit. He accepted the commission, but the trouble was, he didn't write something like the guitar concerto. The piece he wrote for me, called the *Concierto pastoral*, has the most tremendously difficult first movement. It then has a beautiful slow movement, but the last movement, which is very folky, is also quite tricky to play.

I also asked Rodrigo whether he would personally arrange for the flute his *Fantasia para un gentilhombre*, which he had written for the great guitarist Andrés Segovia. He didn't want to do that, but he gave permission for me to do it. So my friend David Overton arranged it, but my management at the time insisted on using my name as the arranger. In fact, though, it was done by David, and it's a very good arrangement indeed.

I had discussed all this with Rodrigo sometime in 1977, and then, as I've mentioned, I went to Spain to do a concert with Marisa Robles early in 1978. I was still in my wheelchair, but I managed to get to Madrid, and there I was met by Marisa and her father. He held an important post in the government, and when they escorted me into the hotel, the people working there bowed down almost to the floor in greeting Marisa's father. But they made it quite clear that Marisa was not allowed to take me to my room, even though I needed someone to push my wheelchair.

Eventually, we got it sorted out. That evening Marisa's father took us to a really terrific Spanish restaurant, and we had a wonderful time. The next day I got ready to go and meet Rodrigo. Marisa, who was helping me with this whole operation, came around and picked me up. We got a taxi, and I transferred myself from the wheelchair to the seat. Meanwhile, the driver and Marisa put the wheelchair on top of the taxi, and off we went. When we arrived at Rodrigo's house, we did the whole thing in reverse—wheelchair off the top of the taxi, me out of the taxi and into the wheelchair—and Marisa wheeled me into Rodrigo's house, where we met the great man himself and his wife.

They were both completely charming, and we had a nice visit. He showed me a little machine that he had for transferring notes onto paper, so that he could record his ideas. He told me that he also had people who helped him do this.

We talked for a while, then he showed me the flute concerto he had written. I couldn't believe my eyes—I mean, I really could not believe how difficult this music was. But I never asked him to change one note of it. I thought, Okay, I shall rise to the challenge, and I shall learn this piece and do it.

And, in fact, we did do it. We gave the world premiere of the *Concierto pastoral* in London, in the Festival Hall, and the BBC filmed it and later showed it on television. That was an amazing evening. The following day, we went to Kingsway Hall and recorded it. The orchestra was the Philharmonia, and the conductor was Eduardo Mata. Rodrigo was present for that, and he stayed while we recorded the *Fantasia para un gentilhombre*. He was so delighted with this recording, he said, "I wish I *had* arranged it, now that I see the possibilities."

For a time I was the only one who played the *Concierto pastoral*, but now a lot of young people play it. Some of my students play it from memory and do a really great job with it.

I then wanted to commission another piece, and it wound up working out even better than I had expected, although for quite a while I thought it wasn't going to happen at all.

This story begins in 1978, while I was working on learning the Rodrigo pieces. Annie and I were still married, and she wanted to go to

Israel to visit her aunt Katya. Katya wasn't actually related to Annie but was a friend of her mother's, and Annie had grown up calling her Aunt Katya. In any case, we went to Israel with our three kids.

Once we got there, I found out that Leonard Bernstein was conducting the Israel Philharmonic. So I decided I'd go along and ask Lenny to write a flute concerto. I went into the hall where they were rehearsing, and there he was, a glass of Scotch in one hand and a cigarette in the other, enjoying life to the fullest. I asked him whether he'd like to write a flute concerto for me, and he said he couldn't because he was already committed to writing one for someone else. There had been a young flute player who was riding a bus one day, and he was shot dead in a terrorist attack. His parents had commissioned a flute concerto from Lenny in their son's memory. But Lenny said to me, "Why don't you get John Corigliano to write a flute concerto?" He had already written two fine wind concertos, one for oboe and the other for clarinet.

I wrote to John, and he wrote back to say that he didn't have a concerto in mind, but if he got an idea, he would give me a call. A year or so later I was in New York, and I went to a party at a friend's house. John was there and Samuel Barber and various other people—I remember that Lynn Harrell, the cellist, was one of the guests.

The first thing that popped into my mind when I saw Sam Barber was, I'll ask *him* to write a flute concerto. I did ask him, but he said that he was too ill. (In fact, he died only a few months later.) He added, "Why don't you try my violin concerto? It's a very nice piece, and it would go great on the flute." I decided to do this.

Yet I also went over to John and asked, "Hey, John! How's my flute concerto coming on?"

John laughed and said, "Listen, if I get an idea, I'll definitely call you."

About six months later, he did call me. "Jimmy," he said, "I've got this great idea—the Pied Piper." John is someone who doesn't write a piece just to write a piece. He writes a piece of theater, and

I love to make music with kids. Here I am rehearsing with some young performers for John Corigliano's Pied Piper Fantasy *with the Baltimore Symphony and David Zinman (not shown) in 1989.*

he imagines it being executed dramatically. So he came up with this Pied Piper idea, based on the Browning poem. It involved my coming onstage as the Pied Piper and then going through the whole story. I play the flute at first, and there's a big cadenza where I kill the rats. Next we have the burghers' chorale. When they don't pay up, I get out my tin whistle and summon a bunch of kids who are planted in the audience to come up on the stage. John had read some of those press accounts about my playing the tin whistle and thought it would work perfectly in this concerto, and it does. We all play the piper's tune, me on the tin whistle and the kids on flutes and drums, and we go marching off to this music, while the orchestra solemnly plays the tune I played when I first came in. It's an incredibly moving piece.

When John was finally ready to write this concerto, he came to Switzerland to meet with me. I remember him calling me up from Bellinzona, saying, "Jimmy! I don't know what to do down here. Nobody speaks English, and I don't know what train to get on."

"John, look at the train," I said. "If it says 'Luzern' on the side of it, get in it." So he did. Fortunately, it was going the right way. I didn't think until afterward that it might have been going *from* Lucerne to Milan. But he was on the right side of the tracks, and he arrived safely.

While he was here, we spent a lot of time together, writing bits and pieces and just playing. John actually wrote the first part of the concerto while he was in Switzerland. Then he went back to the States, and he eventually finished it and sent it to me. I began to practice like a maniac. Then we went on a cruise—it was another of the *Mermoz* cruises. I played my parts of the music for John, and when I had finished, I asked, "What do you think?"

"It's great," he said. "Except this cadenza has to go about twice as fast." Man! I was breaking my fingers as it was, and he wanted it faster? I did get it up to speed, though. And when I listened to the recording later, I was amazed—I didn't think anybody could play like that. But you know, when you're actually doing it, you somehow rise to the occasion of playing this very difficult piece.

We finally got it up and running, and the first performance, in February 1982, was conducted by the wonderful Korean conductor Myung-whun Chung, with the Los Angeles Philharmonic. It was a huge hit, and since then I've played it all over the place, especially with one of my favorite flute-concerto conductors, Leonard Slatkin. And that's how that concerto came to be.

Another very successful commission came about a bit more unconventionally. One day I was walking in New York with my manager at that time, Charlie Hamlin. Charlie is six-foot-something—don't ask me how much, but he's very tall. Whenever I walk along the street with Charlie, I always talk to his left elbow, because it's more convenient than his ear, which is way up in the air above my head.

Anyway, while I was having a chat with Charlie's left elbow, I mentioned that I had heard a flute sonata by Lowell Liebermann that I really enjoyed. I said to Charlie, "You know, we should ask Lowell Liebermann, if he's interested in writing a flute concerto for me before someone else gets the idea of asking him."

Charlie stopped in his tracks, and he said, "Jimmy! This is Lowell Liebermann." He gestured to a man in a T-shirt and, I think, an orange baseball cap who was just a few yards away, walking toward us.

The man stopped to say hi to Charlie, and Charlie said, "Lowell, this is James Galway—Jimmy, this is Lowell Liebermann."

We shook hands, and I said, "Lowell, I really enjoyed your flute sonata. Would you like to write a flute concerto?"

"Sure—why not?" he said.

Even at the time, that seemed to me such a funny way to commission something. Anyway, we conversed a little longer, and then he left, and we walked on about our business. This amazing chance meeting happened across the street from Avery Fisher Hall, just outside Fiorello's restaurant.

Lowell wrote the flute concerto as promised, and I learned it. I have to tell you, it was a really difficult piece to master. We managed to get it programmed with Leonard Slatkin and the St. Louis Symphony. I do think Leonard has conducted more performances of flute concertos than any other conductor alive.

We all went off to St. Louis a few days before the event to get ready. I played the concerto for Lowell, and he told me, "This bit's got to be faster. . . . That bit's got to be slower. . . . This bit has to be like this." We worked it all out, then rehearsed it with Leonard and played the world premiere. It had a *great* reception, I have to say. Since then, it has gone straight into the repertoire—people play it all the time. I was glad to be the one who commissioned it.

Afterward, I also commissioned another piece by Lowell—a flute and harp concerto, which is quite unlike any of his other pieces because it's actually slow. I commissioned this one along with the Na family of Korea. Hyun-Sun Na is the harpist, and her family came in on the commission with me, because I had come to realize that a commission is a bit expensive. But it was worth it: this Liebermann piece was also a great success.

Meanwhile, I liked Sam Barber's suggestion that I should do his violin concerto. It's a beautiful piece of music, and, as he said, it would suit the flute perfectly. So my management got in touch with Eugene Ormandy and the Philadelphia Orchestra, because they had premiered the concerto many years earlier. Mr. Ormandy liked the idea, and we agreed that I would record this piece with them.

But Sam Barber had died before we set this in motion, and his estate simply turned the matter over to the lawyers. What should have been a simple, straightforward project became so complicated that I finally said, "Okay, I ain't gonna do this."

So I rang up Mr. Ormandy, and he decided that we would do the Nielsen instead, along with a Mozart concerto, at Carnegie Hall.

But we would meet in Philadelphia ahead of time and run through the music. I was in New York at the time, so I thought it should be an easy matter to go over to Philadelphia.

I went to Penn Station and found the right train, and the conductor turned out to be a charming fellow. He looked the way a conductor should look, too—well built and sturdy. He asked me what I was going to do in Philadelphia, because he realized when I spoke that I wasn't exactly from around those parts.

I told him, "Well, I'm going to rehearse with Mr. Ormandy for a concert in Carnegie Hall."

"Oh, that's great," he said. After that, he paused to have a word with me whenever he came through the car.

The train trundled along, and eventually we came to the 30th Street station. I thought, Okay, I'll wait and get out at the central station.

Unfortunately, I didn't know at the time that 30th Street *is* the central station in Philadelphia. So the next time the conductor came past, he said, "Hey, I thought you were going to go and play with Mr. Ormandy."

I said, "Yeah, I'm going to wait until we get to the central station."

"Well, that was it—Thirtieth Street," he said.

I thought, in my European way, What a funny name for a central station!

But my conductor friend had an idea: "Here's what we're going to do. We're going to let you out at the next station, even though this train doesn't usually stop there. There's a train coming the other way, and I'll radio them and tell them to pick you up."

And that's what we did. They stopped our train, and I got off. I was the only person standing there on the platform. The other train came along in a few minutes, I boarded it, and soon the conductor came by, and he said, "Oh, you're the fellow who's going to rehearse with Mr. Ormandy."

This is amazing, I thought.

I got off at 30th Street and found a cab, but by then I was sweating like a pig because I was so late. I went along to the Barclay Hotel in Rittenhouse Square, where Mr. Ormandy lived. I felt so hot and bothered—I was even wearing a suit for the occasion.

Mr. Ormandy came to greet me, and he was charming. He asked, "Is there anything I can do for you?"

"Oh, you know," I said, "if I could take a shower, I would be the happiest guy."

"Just a second," Eugene said. "I need to talk to my wife."

He went and spoke with his wife, in German. I heard him say something, and she replied in German, at many more decibels than was necessary, "What?! He wants to take a *shower*? Are you crazy?"

But when Mr. Ormandy came back, he said smoothly, "My wife is just preparing the guest bathroom, because we have some guests and she just needs to clean it up a little bit."

I realized later what had happened. It was actually Mr. Ormandy's bathroom, and it had doors on both ends. So Mrs. Ormandy simply took the clothes and the used towels out of the bathroom and dumped them all in the bedroom, shut the door, and let me in the other door.

I took the shower and felt a lot better. Then we started to rehearse, and this was fun, rehearsing with Mr. Ormandy. When we came to the Mozart concerto, he said, "Listen, you don't need to play the whole concerto—just play the cadenza."

So I started to play the cadenza, and the piano player looked up and said, "Jimmy, this cadenza you're playing is in the wrong key."

"Oh, aren't we doing the G major?" I asked.

"No," he said, "the D major."

I played him the cadenza of the D major, and off I went back to New York. It just so happened that *Amadeus* was playing on Broadway, so I went to see it with my manager, Byron Gustafson. It was terrific. The whole cast was amazing, but especially Ian McKellen as Salieri and Tim Curry as Mozart. We went backstage afterward, and I got Mozart to sign my Nielsen flute concerto.

There were still a few days before the concert. One evening I went to a bar, and there was a guy wearing a yellow jacket, with "Alabama" written on the back. That was the name of a band, which was quite successful at that time.

He was a big, beefy guy, and when I came up and tried to get to the bar, he didn't move an inch. I had to push past him, and I said to him, "Hey, you want to fight?"

He thought this was a huge joke. So we started to talk, and I told him what I did, and he told me what he did—it turned out he was in the band. "I love your jacket," I said.

"Man, it's yours," he said, and he took off the jacket and gave it to me. I put it on over the clothes I was wearing, but it was still miles too big. Meanwhile, I told him he should come to our concert.

After a couple of drinks, I went to my hotel and climbed into bed. About one in the morning, the phone rang. It was my new friend's girlfriend, and she said, "Hey, listen—I've got to get something out of the pocket of the jacket that my man gave you."

"What?" I asked.

"I think he left his stash in there," she said.

She came around to collect it, and I gave her back the jacket as well.

The next evening, he did come to the concert, and it was a riot. The way the Mozart concerto goes, after the first entry of the flute, I play alone a bit. When I finished doing my thing, this guy applauded and yelled, "Hey, great!" the way you would at a rock concert, when somebody does a riff.

Anyway, that didn't spoil the concerto, and it was an enormous success. When we had finished playing, everyone kept on applauding, so I finally said to the audience—well, I didn't say it, I *yelled* it—"We're going to play the last movement for you again."

It was at this point that I realized Mr. Ormandy didn't hear so well, because he asked, "*What* are we going to do?"

I said, "Well, I just told the audience we're going to play the last movement again."

"Oh, fine," he said, and off we went and did it again.

That was my first time playing with Eugene Ormandy. I came to know him quite well, and once Mrs. Ormandy got over her shock at my request for a shower, she proved to be a lovely woman. They really were the nicest couple.

I've tried to think of a way to pull all of this together, in describing the way I relate to music. First, I'd like to say that a lot depends on what you're playing at the moment. You've got to get inside the music that you're playing right now. Let's say you're doing a Beethoven symphony. For that moment in your life, that symphony is the greatest piece in the world. Or let's say you're in the opera, and you happen to be doing something as daft as *The Mikado*. For the couple of hours that you're playing it, you need to feel that it's the greatest piece. In each case, you burrow right down in and learn all the little things the composer indulged in to make it what it is.

Having said that, I'll add that if I had to choose a single favorite composer, it would definitely be Beethoven. This is true even though he wrote so little for the solo flute. But I love the symphonies, the string quartets, the piano concertos, the piano sonatas, the violin sonatas, and of course his little flute piece, the Serenade, opus 25, which I recorded a while back. Some people say that Beethoven is particularly difficult, but I don't find that he's any harder to play than any other composer. Whether it's Beethoven's *Pastoral* Symphony, which has a nice flute part, or *L'Après-midi d'un faune*, or "The Pink Panther," for that matter, you have to first get inside the spirit of the music. Let's say you're going to play or sing in the Mozart *Requiem*. This is a majestic piece, and you have to channel your thoughts into some sort of respect—the same type of respect you would have if you went into a church and prayed. In fact, when you listen to the beginning of the Mozart *Requiem*, it actually sounds as if it's in church, even if you're playing it in your little room at home. Mozart

This may look like I'm having a serious musical conversation with Sir Neville Marriner, but we were probably comparing notes on the quality of the wine.

was a believer, and I think he wrote this mass really intending to glorify God. So when you play music like this, you have to play it with reverence. Whereas if you're playing the Scherzo from the Ninth Symphony, that's a really happy, up-tempo, energetic piece, and you galvanize all of your energy to do it.

Whatever you're playing, you have to prepare yourself, physically and mentally. I've mentioned that my recovery from the accident brought me back to God, and now I pray before every concert, and Jeanne prays with me if she's there. We thank God for the talent He has given us and ask Him to get us into the spirit of the evening and to help us to walk in His ways. This brings me back to the physical preparation. If you're given a talent like this, you have a duty to look after it. You have to nourish it and work on it, so that you can use it to the very best of your ability. I think this is what I do with my flute playing.

Of course, I enjoy playing the flute, and I think the fact that I enjoy it comes out when I play. This was true even before I started my solo career. I really loved playing the Beethoven symphonies when I was in the Berlin Philharmonic, and things like the *Symphonie Fantastique* of Berlioz. Even if other instruments have more to do, your little part in the orchestra will shine if you enjoyed preparing for it and you enjoy playing it.

Actually, it has been a very rare occasion when I haven't liked playing a particular piece of music. I've mentioned a couple of the modern works we did back when I was with the Royal Philharmonic, in which I could never find any melodic sense. Some of the modern music we did in Berlin was a bit far-fetched, too, and not many of those works have ever come into the general repertoire of the major symphony orchestras. But we played them anyway in Berlin and gave those composers a chance. I think that's the correct thing to do, because although I'm rather old-fashioned, and I love Beethoven, Mozart, Haydn, Brahms, Schubert, Mahler, all of those guys, I do enjoy listening to modern music as well.

Recently, I paid a visit to the Paris Conservatoire flute class of Sophie Cherrier. A young woman named Charlotte Bletton played a piece written by a Japanese composer, Fuminori Tanada, and it was just so beautiful. She enjoyed doing it—you could hear that she got a real kick out of playing this. I think the composer had fun writing it, too, and it was a well-thought-out piece. It was called "F," after his own first name, Fuminori.

In a Prom concert on TV, I heard a piece called "Helix," written by Esa-Pekka Salonen of the Los Angeles Philharmonic. I thought, This is a pretty good piece; I think Mr. Salonen should write a flute concerto. You can watch "Helix" on YouTube.

A few months ago I made a recording with the group Tiempo Libre, led by pianist Jorge Gomez. These young people are Cubans, now living in the United States. They're all classically trained, and their Afro-Cuban jazz is just terrific. We recorded Claude Bolling's jazz suites, originally recorded by Jean-Pierre Rampal, along with a couple of new pieces by Jorge. We called the record *O'Reilly Street*, because I got a kick out of the Irish-Cuban connection: an important battle in the Cuban War of Independence was won by an Irishman, General O'Reilly, and a major street in Havana is named after him.

When I was in Ireland recently, I had the most fantastic time. I was there to perform with the orchestra of the Irish national broadcasting company, RTE, conducted by Gerhard Markson. The orchestra was going to play two concerts, and I was the soloist in one of them. The first one I merely listened to, in the National Concert Hall in Dublin. I got to hear Beethoven's Ninth and the Mozart A Major Piano Concerto—it was simply magnificent. The symphony was well played and well sung—the four soloists were wonderful—and the piano concerto was beautifully played by a young Irishman, Finghin Collins. Two days later, we all went to Limerick to play there. In the second half of my concert, the orchestra played Beethoven's Seventh. What a wonderful experience it was to hear two great Beethoven symphonies in the same week. It was a particular treat to hear them led by a good German conductor, Gerhard Markson, and outstandingly played by the National Orchestra of Ireland. Lyric FM, which is the classical-music station of RTE, hosted the whole thing, in celebration of its tenth birthday. I was very happy to be part of it all.

Markson had kicked off that second concert with a piece written by a young woman named Elaine Agnew. I thought, Boy, this is a really good, well-structured piece. The audience enjoyed it, too. I met the composer afterward, and it turns out she is from Belfast, my hometown. We had a bit of a talk, and I think she's going to write a new flute concerto, which I will be very happy to play. And besides the coincidence of our both coming from Belfast, she told me that her cousin John works in a watch shop in Lucerne.

It's difficult to say what will become of classical music, but I don't think it will come to an end, the way some people predict, because young composers today have really changed how audiences listen to music. I used to be one of those skeptics who said that to get people to listen to new music, you'd have to pay them. And not so long ago, this was true: when you put on a piece of modern music, nobody came. But now people are actually coming to hear it. My friend John Corigliano, who wrote the *Pied Piper Fantasy* for me, wrote an opera, *The Ghosts of Versailles*, and I heard they were scalping tickets outside the doors when the Metropolitan Opera put it on in New York. Deutsche Grammophon made a video of it, and I bought a copy, and I think it's terrific. When you begin any new endeavor, you think, I wonder how this is going to go on. But suddenly you find yourself engrossed with the whole project.

Other friends of mine, like Lowell Liebermann and William Bolcom, have written wonderful flute concertos—these guys are truly masters of the craft. When I play their concertos, the audience absolutely loves them, and this, too, is modern music.

The last word on classical music is that there are children all over the world playing strings and woodwinds, and they are playing classical music. So no matter what people in the media say, classical music is not dead.

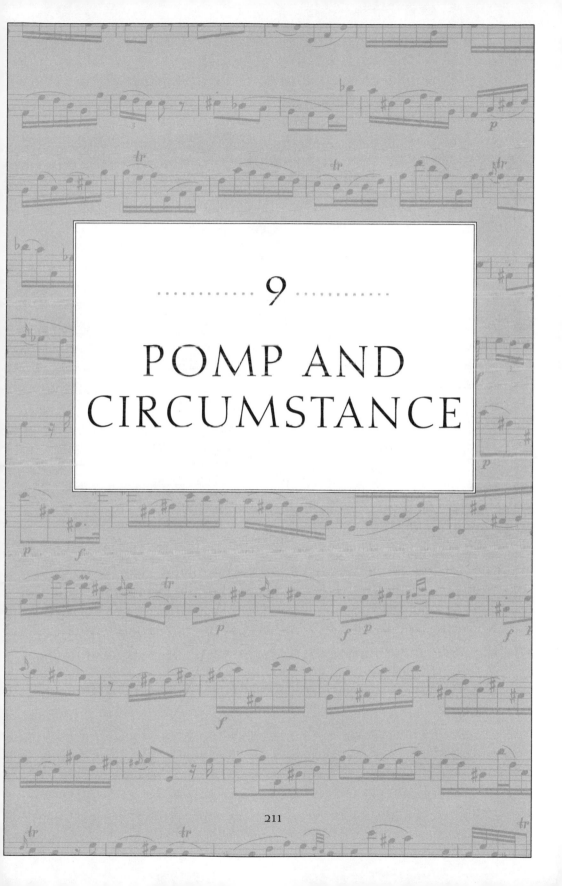

9

POMP AND CIRCUMSTANCE

I N THE COURSE OF TOOTING MY FLUTE, I'VE BEEN
privileged to meet some pretty impressive people. I've already
mentioned quite a few of them in the world of music, but
what I want to recall now are kings, queens, presidents, and all that.
We'll start with July 1991, when I went to the best party I've ever
attended in my life. This was at Buckingham Palace, in the interior
courtyard. It was in connection with the G7 summit that was taking
place in London at the time.

The evening started off with a piper standing right up on the top
of the palace, where the flag is usually flying. I didn't recognize the
tune he played, but it was a slow lament, and it was very moving.
Then came the bands. To kick things off down at ground level, the
band of the Household Cavalry rode in and played the minuet from
The Marriage of Figaro. This was in honor of the two-hundredth
anniversary of Mozart's death. It was beautifully done. The horses
seemed to be waltzing to this minuet in 3/4 time. Then came all
sorts of other bands, like the Welsh Guards, the Irish Guards, the

Scots Guards, the Grenadier Guards, the Navy Band, the Air Force Band—all of these bands were playing together, with yours truly in front of them.

We had rehearsed this earlier in the week at the Chelsea Barracks in London. It was a bright, sunny day, and the huge parade ground was crowded with musicians as far as the eye could see. Because this was for the G7 summit, one of the pieces I was going to play was an arrangement of "If I Were a Rich Man." But when I was given my music, I saw that some prankster in one of the bands had changed the title on the first page to "Now I Am a Rich Man."

One thing about this rehearsal that really struck me was that all of these were military bands, yet nobody seemed to pay any attention to rank. The atmosphere was very easygoing. When the director of music spoke to the men, however, there was silence, and they followed his instructions to the letter.

There was a sergeant who was assigned to show me the ropes and set me up to do the job. He said, "Listen, Jimmy, during the entrance, when we are marching in, whatever you do, don't stop. This is a marching machine, and these guys will walk right over you. Don't look right or left. Just march." So, here I was marching again—but this was a far cry from the Onward Flute Band or the 39th Old Boys.

We started with the musical rehearsal, and when we played "Danny Boy," I asked the director, "Oh, can we do a little rallentando here?"

He replied, "No, we don't do rallentandos. By the time the rallentando went all the way through from the front to the back, and back up here, we'd be in a different place altogether. So we will play it like a march." So that was "Danny Boy" for you, British-military-band style. But it was fun.

At one point, tea was delivered to us in large white plastic containers of the type they use for benzene or gasoline. We were all drinking tea out of these containers, and I'm not going to tell you some of the jokes the boys made about the color of the tea.

Then the evening came for the actual performance at Buckingham Palace.

At the appointed time, the lights went out, and I was ushered to my spot in front of all the bands, up there with the drum major, who gives the tempo and keeps them all marching in time. The lights came back on, and we started marching along. Then we stopped at a prearranged place, a spotlight shone on me, and a voice said, "Ladies and gentlemen, Mr. James Galway."

I started to play the two tunes we had rehearsed, and a beautiful laser light show accompanied the music, moving around the courtyard. Then the bands played the national anthem of each of the seven countries represented, and there was a light show appropriate to each of the anthems. After the national anthems, there were incredible fireworks.

When the fireworks were over, I was ushered toward the palace itself, where I would attend the reception given by the queen. I had to go past the members of the press, who were all sitting there. I knew half of them, and they teased me as I walked past in my white suit, which I'd had made specially for the occasion. Then we came to the door that I was supposed to enter, and wouldn't you know? It was locked. The gentleman who was looking after me made a rather pungent Anglo-Saxon comment and then led me back again to try another entrance. This meant I had to pass the press again, and they gave me another ribbing.

The next door worked, and my minder led me through corridors lined with office after office. This was very interesting, because I hadn't realized what a truly big business the monarchy is. Just the Duke of Edinburgh's charity alone is huge, and then there are all the other charities that are run from the palace. The royals are very generous with their time and money.

The other thing that struck me as we walked through these corridors was the prints on the walls depicting all the battles the British have been involved in. I recognized Waterloo and a few others, but there were dozens more. Someday, I would like to simply walk around and look at them all properly.

Eventually, we made our way to the main hall and then up the stairs. As I entered the reception hall, Queen Elizabeth was talking with a tall, pleasant-looking man. When she spotted me, she said, "Jimmy! Do you know Mr. Mulroney?"

So I said to the prime minister of Canada, "No. Very pleased to meet you. Sorry I'm late—we got locked out."

The queen thought this was a good one, being locked out of the palace. According to the briefing I'd been given, I was supposed to be presented to the queen first. But when I did not appear on schedule, the palace attendants must have figured there was something amiss. They had proceeded to plan B and begun to present the G7 representatives.

The queen has always been very kind to me, starting with that Saint Cecilia's Day concert in 1976 with Marisa Robles, my all-time favorite harp player. One little sidelight of that day was that when Marisa and I were presented to the queen and the Duke of Edinburgh, the former head of the Royal College of Music, Sir Keith Falkner, was also there. I had been the black sheep of the Royal College, because I had left there to go to the Guildhall to study with Geoffrey Gilbert, and that sort of thing definitely was not done. I am sure Sir Keith had heard all about this from some of the people in the college when he took over from Sir Ernest Bullock, who had been the director when I made my famous move. So that day in the royal box, Sir Keith had to bite the bullet and be nice to me. However, he did a good job, I must say—he was very diplomatic.

I've met the queen several times since then, most memorably, of course, when she gave me my knighthood. Altogether, I've played many times for her and for various other members of the royal family. During one week, I met the Queen Mother twice. One of these occasions was a concert I did with Marisa in a well-known church near the Houses of Parliament, St. John's, Smith Square, which is the

Meeting the queen backstage after the Royal Variety Performance in 1979, at the Theatre Royal, Drury Lane. Bill Haley is on my right, and Red Buttons is on my left.

venue for many wonderful concerts. It is a beautiful church and one of the best examples of English Baroque, built in 1728.

I was invited to the special tribute to the Queen Mother at the Palladium in 1980. Concerts at the Palladium are always outstanding, because of the level of talent they attract.

I remember the first time I played at Buckingham Palace. The queen wasn't there, but Prince Charles was—the concert was being given for one of the charities that he organized—and I was playing with Phillip Moll. I couldn't help noticing that one of the guests, a woman in a green dress, was showing more than is customary at Buckingham Palace, and she was smoking during the concert. It was clear that she had absolutely no idea what sort of behavior is expected at the palace or what classical music is all about; I could only suppose that her husband or boyfriend had a ton of money and was prepared to give a chunk of it to Prince Charles's charity.

Still, we had a fun time at that little gathering, and afterward we were all shown into the dining room. That was simply the most amazing scene you can imagine. The tables were all lit by candles in dazzling candelabra, and the table was set with Queen Victoria's dinner service. I thought I was attending a formal dinner in a novel by Tolstoy or Dostoyevsky.

Suddenly, there was consternation among the palace staff. They had thought that Phillip's page turner, a Japanese lady, was only the page turner—hired help, so to speak—and that she would leave as soon as we were finished playing. To their horror, she started to come into the dining room with us, and only then did the staff discover that she was Phillip's brand-new wife. It was too late to rearrange the main table, but someone thought quickly. They put a little table on the side, where Phillip and Yuko had the most romantic dinner.

Another thing—we had flown to London from the south of England in a private plane that day. I wondered whether Yuko thought this was the kind of extravagance we indulged in all the time. But you know, sometimes you just can't get where you need to be quickly enough any other way, and you have to hire a private plane to fly you there, even though it cuts into the profits. Never mind—if it matters to you, that's what you do.

I once played at a very different sort of event, a concert benefiting a school. It was a quasi-amateur orchestra; quite a few of my friends were playing in it as principals and leaders, but the rest of the orchestra consisted of lawyers and such, and Prince Charles was playing the cello. They had engaged me to play the Bach B Minor Suite. While I was waiting to go on, I was looking through one of the rooms, which had some wonderful first editions of English writers. I was reveling in all these priceless treasures when Prince Charles walked into the room. He looked at me and said with a smile, "Have you heard the orchestra?"

"Unfortunately, yes," I replied. He thought this was a hoot. Even as an amateur cellist, he could appreciate how far from perfection they all were. I have to say, though, it was a great evening, and I was happy to be with my friends and to make a little bit of money for the charity we were all working so hard to support.

By the way, I have two all-time ambitions: one is to look at the queen's stamp collection, and the other is to get locked up in her wine cellar for about a month, with a bed, a glass, and a corkscrew.

I have also played for most of the U.S. presidents over the last thirty years. Let me start at the beginning, with Jimmy Carter.

I met President Carter the day after John Lennon was killed—which happened, by what to me was an odd coincidence, on my forty-first birthday, December 8, 1980. I was about to go to the White House when Jeanne called me from New York. We were good friends by that time, though we hadn't become, so to speak, an item. But she thought I should know the bad news. She told me there was a big crowd of people gathering in front of the Dakota, across the street from where she lived, and she had heard people saying that someone had shot John Lennon. That was a downer for me—I was and still am a big fan of the Beatles and their music.

The reason I happened to be in Washington was to play at the Kennedy Center. The occasion was the annual event at which they give out the Kennedy Center Lifetime Achievement Awards. One of the honorees that year was James Cagney, whom I had watched many times at the cinema as a kid. I especially remembered his gangster pictures and also *Yankee Doodle Dandy*, which I loved. Cagney had requested that I be there when he was honored and that I play "Danny Boy." Then President Carter invited all of us—the honorees, their families, and the people who had provided the entertainment—to the White House the next day.

I never met Ronald Reagan. I was in Washington a few times while he was in office, especially for those Fourth of July celebrations, but I didn't play at the White House during his presidency. Yet I had a curious brush with some of his people.

It was in the mid-eighties, and President Reagan was planning to meet with Chairman Gorbachev on a ship off the coast of Finland. This didn't work out because of bad weather, so it was arranged that they would meet instead in the concert house in Helsinki, right after a series of concerts in which I was playing. One day Jeanne and I were walking down the street in Helsinki, and two men walked toward us. One of them said, "Good afternoon, Mr. Galway."

"Hello," I said. "Who are you?"

"My name's Robert White," he said, "and I work at the White House."

"But have we met?" I didn't recognize him, and I have a pretty good memory for faces.

"No, I'm security," he replied, "but I've seen you playing on television."

"What are you doing here?" I asked.

He said, "Oh, we're just checking it out—you know, for terrorists and stuff like that."

I thought this was amazing—that the White House would send its security agents all the way from Washington to check out the situation before the president got there.

The concert hall was basically taken to pieces by these security guys—the CIA or the FBI or the GPO or whoever they were. I heard that they disabled the entire telephone system and put their own system in. As soon as we finished our last concert, we were required to leave the building immediately, so that they could get on with their work. It was a very big operation, and it gave me a little glimpse of what goes on when such a meeting of world leaders is planned.

That's what I remember about President Reagan, apart from the fact that I always thought he was a jolly fellow, and he did a good job of bringing down the Wall in Berlin.

A few years later, I was playing in a Christmas concert in Washington, and George and Barbara Bush came to it. It was 1989, their first Christmas in the White House. They invited the principal performers to come back there with them for drinks. So we went to the White House, and they showed us around the place, the Oval Office and everything.

George and Barbara were such a cute couple. At one point, George was explaining to us all his TV equipment—there were a dozen TVs all playing at once, and if he saw something that took his fancy, he would click on it to bring up the sound. Then Barbara interjected, "Except he never knows how it works." Man, I thought, the president of the United States is like every other guy in the world—he loves his gadgets, but he doesn't really know how to work them. When I think about it now, I am sure this was not strictly true, but it was funny at the time.

Barbara gave us a special tour of the White House. She showed us the bedroom where Lincoln slept and all sorts of other historical items. There was a huge Christmas tree, and Mrs. Bush told us, "You know, when we moved into the White House, of course it was January, but the first thing the staff wanted to know about was the

Christmas tree." It seems that the tree always has a particular theme. So she had plenty of time to think about the theme of the Bushes' first White House Christmas tree, and the theme that she chose was literacy, a cause she has championed ever since. The tree was hung with hundreds of little books.

Meanwhile, Barbara explained to us that there are tons of pictures stored in the basement, and each new president and first lady choose what they want to hang. She pointed out some of the pictures she and George had decided on. I remember that she had one room in which all the pictures were of women who had some connection with the White House—the first girl born there, the first set of twins born there, the first young woman married there, and so on. There was one picture of a lady with a very heavy five-o'clock shadow, and Barbara remarked, "Can you imagine how discreet the painter had to be to get it to look as light as this?"

Then she showed us a carpet she had started to make when she and George were living in China. George wasn't technically the ambassador, because the United States didn't recognize China at that time, but he was the chief U.S. representative. Anyway, this carpet was amazing—Barbara had attended a carpet-making class in China, and her work was beautiful. It was a blue carpet, and the general motif was birds. She finished it after they returned to the United States, and I believe she incorporated a reference to her first grandchild.

The next president I had the pleasure to meet was Bill Clinton, and he was a riot. As I've said, I don't particularly follow the news, but I think he was a people's president, because he really reached out to the public. He also tried to do something about the situation in Northern Ireland, which was dear to my heart. What he did, which was remarkable, was to send former senator George Mitchell to Belfast, to oversee the truce negotiations on a daily basis. During the months Mitchell spent on this difficult and dangerous job, off and on over several years, he lived in the Europa Hotel in Belfast, which is owned by my friend Sir William Hastings. Back during the Troubles, it was the most-bombed hotel in the world—it was bombed more than thirty times, and Sir William was kidnapped by the IRA twice. Eventually, though, the efforts of Mitchell and others did lead to peace, or at least to a truce that seems to have held.

Anyway, the first time I played at the White House during the Clinton years, in March 1997, the president himself was not in the audience. He wanted to come down and hear us play, but he couldn't, because he had recently damaged a tendon in his knee. So we went up to the family quarters and spoke with him for about twenty minutes. We mostly talked about music. He played the saxophone—quite well, I think—and he told us he was going to South America for a meeting and was looking forward to listening to the local jazz while he was there.

The following year I went to the White House for a St. Patrick's Day reception, and it was a wonderful occasion. The Clintons had decorated everything to look as Irish as possible. That day the White House could have been called the Green House. Bill Clinton was making a point of saluting the Irish on their national day for what they had done for the U.S.A. After all, ten American presidents had Irish roots, the first one being Andrew Jackson, whose people came from around where I grew up.

At the beginning of the evening, we were all waiting in line to be presented to the president and the first lady. The Clintons arrived, and when Bill came to me, he shook hands and said, "Ah, Your Eminence! Remember I told you I was going to South America and hoped to listen to some jazz? Well, everybody got enthusiastic, and they took me to this nightclub where there was a female jazz singer on the bill. I thought I was going to see some wonderful sexy singer. Then in came this three-hundred-pound dumpy little chick, and she sang the roof off the place."

The next time I was invited to the White House, it was to play for George W. Bush. That was another St. Patrick's Day, but it was nothing at all like the party the Clintons had laid on. However,

It was truly a pleasure to greet President Bill Clinton before I performed for him and honored guests at the White House on St. Patrick's Day in 1998.

I have to say that President Bush was charming, and he really enjoyed our music. I was playing with Jay Ungar and Molly Mason, the folk-music duo. We did songs like "Presidential Hornpipes," which were written to commemorate some of the United States' more brilliant presidents. We had wanted to play the "West Texas Waltz," but were told by the White House staff that it was too long. I thought at the time that we should have gone ahead and played it, because George W. seemed to be enjoying himself.

This year, 2009, we met the president of Israel, Shimon Peres. That was a very special event—once we finally made it through the security screening.

We had arrived in a taxi at the president's house, and a young woman at the security station looked at me and asked, "Are you a terrorist?" (I wondered at the time whether this was some sort of Israeli joke, but I couldn't see the humor of it.)

"No," I said.

She asked, "Are you carrying any weapons?" (Another joke?)

"No," I said.

"Well, walk through there," she said. So I passed through the metal detector.

Now, can you imagine asking questions like that? "Are you a terrorist?" I wanted to say, "Of course I'm a terrorist! Do I have any weapons? Yeah, I've got this flute, and I'm going to take everyone hostage by playing upon it." On reflection, the questions about weapons were probably aimed at members of the Israeli army who might be attending a function, but it still seems daft to ask them of a civilian.

In any case, I was eventually allowed in, and once we were inside the president's house, the atmosphere was very relaxed and informal.

At the reception, a young Israeli girl was playing the recorder, accompanied by her teacher at the harpsichord. She was a wonderful musician and played with a virtuosity that denoted hours of practice. After the reception, we were invited to tea. I was seated beside Mr. Peres, and he spoke about music and whatnot. I told him what I was playing in my concerts with the Israel Chamber Orchestra.

I was very glad to be there, because I hadn't been back to Israel for years, and this gave me a chance to see lots of old friends. I was also able to teach at the local music school in Jerusalem, and I really enjoyed it. I told Mr. Peres that if I were a young man looking to settle somewhere, I might well choose Israel. Because despite everything you read in the newspapers, that nation has such a great atmosphere. I particularly enjoyed Jerusalem; this was the first time I had stayed there long enough to get to know it a bit. What a rich heritage there is to be seen everywhere! I don't want to sound like a travel agent, but I would recommend a visit there to anyone.

Japan is another country that Jeanne and I love to visit. We have many, many friends in Japan, and we've always had a great time there.

I first went to Japan with the Berlin Philharmonic nearly forty years ago, and I've toured there every two years during my career as a soloist. An enormous number of people in Japan play the flute and love listening to flute music. A few years ago, a Swiss photographer, Beat Pfändler, included me in some photos he took for Swissair, and he then used some of those shots for an exhibition he put on in EXPO 2005, in Aichi, Japan. I was told by a friend of mine, the Italian flutist Andrea Griminelli, that at the EXPO, many Japanese people stood beside my picture so as to have *their* picture taken with *my* picture. I love the thought of all those Japanese households with these dual portraits on display.

Some while ago when I was touring in Japan, I met a gentleman named Christopher McDonald. Chris is now retired, but for many years he was the president of Rolex Japan. Japan has an unusual celebration called Time Memorial Day, which is on June 10. It commemorates the bringing of the first clock to Japan from China centuries ago. In the late 1980s, Chris and his colleagues were trying to think of ways to popularize the Rolex brand in Japan, and they hit on the idea of sponsoring a concert on Time Day. They've done this for twenty years now, and these events are hugely popular. Chris asked me to do the Time Day concert in 1993 and again in 2005. On each occasion, I played a flute-and-piano recital with Phillip Moll, and both times we played at Suntory Hall to sold-out houses. The Japanese have a knack for building great concert halls, and Suntory Hall is one of the very best in the world.

A bonus from our first Time Day recital was that I came to know the Irish ambassador to Japan, Jim Sharkey. Now this is an interesting thing. During my entire career, I don't think I've ever been invited to the British embassy in any of the countries I've toured in around the world. (I must add, however, that at home in Switzerland, I was invited to the British embassy in Bern to celebrate the birthday of the queen.) But the Irish ambassadors always invite me. I guess if you're Irish, you may come into the parlor, as the comic song has it—and if you talk like me, you *are* Irish. So you're accepted by the Irish embassy, no matter which part of Ireland you're from.

Anyway, it was Jim Sharkey who first took me to meet the Empress of Japan. Jeanne and I were turned out in our best togs, and Jim picked us up in a big car and drove us to the emperor's palace. It is a splendid building in the middle of Tokyo, and it is visited every day by many Japanese and by tourists from the world over. A lot of men were guarding the gates, but they didn't seem to be armed, except for those long sticks the Japanese use for martial arts. I thought, Well, I don't know what these guys would do if someone approached them with a Kalashnikov. But they were all very helpful to us and showed us where to go. Everyone bowed when we approached.

We had been invited to tea, and I had been asked to bring my flute, which I did. The empress explained that she had prepared some pieces on the piano, and she wanted me to play the flute with her. I remember we played "Annie's Song," and "The Dance of the Blessed Spirits" from Glück's *Orpheus and Eurydice*. The empress had prepared these pieces thoroughly and accompanied me extremely well.

Then we talked with the empress over tea, and she seemed to be very pleased to meet Jeanne. The tea itself was what you might call minimalist—it wasn't the sort of tea you'd get at the Ritz, with scones and clotted cream and all that. It was very Japanese, just a beautiful cup of green tea and some little rice cookies.

As for the palace, it's not like any palace I have ever seen in Britain, Europe, India, or anywhere else. It is simplicity in every sense of the word. In the room where the empress received us, there were no pictures, no books, no prints of famous battles, no sword of the emperor's father hanging on the wall—no mementoes of any kind. It was all very, very simple and, again, very Japanese.

We talked for half an hour, maybe forty minutes—the empress had studied in the United States and England and speaks excellent English—and then we said good-bye. It was a charming afternoon.

The next time we were invited to the palace, Jim Sharkey had moved on to another ambassadorial post, and his successor, Declan O'Donovan, accompanied us. Again I played some songs with the empress, and we had tea.

This time, the empress began to talk to Jeanne on a more personal level. "May I call you Jeannie?" she asked. Of course, Jeanne was over the moon. It was hard for me to talk to her at all after her being on first-name terms with the empress. Throughout this conversation, every ten minutes or so a lady-in-waiting appeared and said something to the empress, who dismissed her. Eventually, after nearly two hours, the empress gave in to the lady-in-waiting, and we all stood up to take our leave.

The empress and some of the palace staff came to the door and waved and bowed to us as we drove off in our spotlessly clean and shining black limousine.

When Phillip and I played our second Time Memorial Day recital for Rolex, we didn't get to see the empress. However, the emperor's brother turned up with an entire entourage from the royal household.

When I came out onto the platform, someone warned me, "Jimmy, you have to bow and acknowledge the presence of the emperor's brother." This is standard in any country that has royalty, so it seemed perfectly normal to me. But I wasn't expecting what happened in the intermission: the emperor's brother led the whole group backstage, and someone took pictures of us. The emperor's brother smoked all the way through the picture-taking session. He remarked to Chris McDonald, "You know, Chris, I see more of my family at a flute recital than I do at dinner." I got a kick out of that.

Another special occasion in Japan is the anniversary celebration for Suntory Hall. I've played twice for that annual celebration. The second time—I think it was for the twentieth anniversary—was a wonderful occasion. The Tokyo Philharmonic Orchestra was playing, and the conductor was Michiyoshi Inoue. He is Japan's leading conductor, and it was a great pleasure to play with him.

I played in the first half, and then I said to Jeanne, "I'd like to stay for the second half—this orchestra is terrific." So we managed to find a pair of seats in the audience.

The program included the chorus from the last movement of the Beethoven Ninth—the "Ode to Joy." I said, "Hey, look at this, Jeannie—all in Japanese." Not only that, there was "Land of Hope and Glory," also in Japanese. I thought, I'm probably the only person in the whole building who can actually say "*Freude,*" rolling the *r* in the proper German way.

"Do we have to stand up and sing this?" I asked Jeanne.

She said, "Yeah, I think that's what we're supposed to do." Of course, Jeanne was putting me on—she's great at leg pulling, my wife is.

Anyway, they played the last movement of the symphony, and it was great—a fantastic tempo. I just loved it.

Then they began to do "Land of Hope and Glory," and this is where I came into my own. Because when we sing it in the Proms, after the line that goes, "Make thee mightier yet," we interject, "Cor blimey!" And I was the only one in that auditorium in Tokyo who gave them the real, authentic "Cor blimey!"—Irish accent and all. The Japanese sitting around me that evening learned something about traditional English music. It is very nice to be able to spread the knowledge of the true interpretation of a good old English standard.

In looking into the history of this magnificent concert hall, I was interested to learn that Herbert von Karajan had had something to do with its planning. He recommended to the designers that the seating be arranged in tiers surrounding the orchestra, something like the design of his own Philharmonie. He also helped with the acoustical evaluation once the hall was completed, and he pronounced it "outstanding." The sentence from his letter that the directors of Suntory Hall love to quote is: "It is truly a jewel box of sound."

Meanwhile, playing with the orchestra in that great concert was my old friend Karl Leister, who had been first clarinet in the Berlin Philharmonic when I was there. He was a wonderful player, and he still is. I can't believe he plays this well at his age. But then again, he can't believe I play this well at my age.

I played a similar concert with Michiyoshi Inoue and the Osaka Philharmonic a few days later, and this time I was the only foreigner on the program. Inoue told me he was going to Moscow to conduct all the Shostakovich symphonies, and I was wishing he would take me with him.

The Empress of Japan did not attend that concert, but she has appeared again in our lives—not in Japan, but in Ireland. Jeanne and I were playing in Dublin, and we got a message from the lord mayor of Dublin. He said that the emperor and empress were in town, and he was giving a reception for them. The empress had learned that we were also in Dublin, and she had asked him if he would invite us. We were very pleased to accept, and we didn't really think about the schedule.

The problem was that we had to fly to Denmark to do a radio show. Not until that morning did I realize that if we went to the reception, we would miss our plane. So I called up the lord mayor's office in a panic, and his secretary said, "Don't worry, Sir James. We shall take care of it."

He explained that what we needed to do was bring our luggage with us and have the taxi driver come around to the front of the mansion house and wait for us there. So we did that, and we were ushered into the reception room. The empress was as charming as we had remembered her. She talked with me for about five minutes, holding my hand the entire time—which I have to say startled me a bit. I'm not used to holding hands with the Empress of Japan.

It was a lovely meeting, and the emperor proved to be as gracious as his wife. And I met more famous Irish people on that one afternoon than I'd ever met in my whole life.

Too soon, Jeanne and I were whisked away to catch our flight. When we came out, two policemen on motorcycles were waiting for us. One policeman said to our taxi driver, "Follow me, and when you get to the Malahide Road, put your emergency lights on."

But we started off very slowly, and I said to Jeanne, "You know what? We're going to miss the plane. I had a police escort once in England, and we went so slowly I nearly missed the concert."

Of course, it wasn't like that at all. When we got to the Malahide Road, our two policemen took off like a shot and stopped all the traffic at the first roundabout. We just sailed right through to the next roundabout, where policeman number one stopped the traffic while policeman number two led us through. Then policeman number two went on ahead and stopped the traffic at the next roundabout, while policeman number one led us through. We got to the airport in twenty minutes, and Jeanne remarked, "Well, I knew you were famous, but this is really impressive." So that's what you have to do if you want to impress your wife.

The lord mayor's thoughtfulness didn't stop there. A fellow from his staff had come with us, and this gentleman took us to someone from the diplomatic corps, who was waiting for us. He in turn introduced us to a giant of a man, who turned out to be the chief of security for Dublin Airport. He led us to the security area and said to the screeners, "This is Sir James and Lady Galway." We put our luggage on the conveyor belt and went bang straight through without anyone questioning us. I was very grateful, but I also thought it was a tremendous pity that you need to have the personal intervention of the lord mayor and the chief of security to avoid being asked a bunch of really dumb questions.

This adventure in Dublin reminds me of the most beautiful president I've ever met, Mary McAleese, the president of Ireland. Mrs. McAleese was born in Belfast, and she is the first Irish president to come from Northern Ireland. We met her one day with a bunch of kids from Belfast, and we had the most wonderful day with her. We all went to Dublin Castle, got our pictures taken, and had tea. Madam President was very charming to everyone and made us feel at home, which, of course, we all were.

10

THE FLUTE
AND ME

THE FLUTE IS A VERY LARGE PART OF MY LIFE. I love playing the flute. I enjoy hearing people play it and listening to recordings of it and talking about it with other flute players. I love it as much now as I did sixty-plus years ago in Belfast, when I became intrigued with it as a youngster—I probably enjoy it a lot more, actually, because I play it so much better now.

Of course, I still practice every day. I enjoy that, too, because there's nothing like doing something well. Now, it's a great advantage to have a good technique that you've built up from childhood, but you still have to maintain this technique. You can't just live on what you were able to do in the past. People who don't play an instrument may think that practicing is simply a matter of learning new pieces or brushing up a piece you haven't played in a while. But it also requires keeping in shape physically. If you draw a comparison, for example, with a ballet dancer who was brilliant when he was twenty-one, he will still be brilliant when he's thirty-one—barring injury—yet he has to practice *every day*.

Some days I wake up, and my playing is not so good. But then I just start in practicing, and eventually I succeed, and I think, Wow! Great! Life is worth it again. It's sort of like people who play golf. I don't mean professionals like Arnold Palmer or Tiger Woods, but just ordinary golfers I've known. They don't play to compete against other people. They play to make themselves better at doing it, better at finding the soul of the game.

Pianists, when they tour, have to play whatever instrument the management provides, but most instrumentalists bring their own. That's certainly the case with flutists. Over the years, I have acquired many flutes, and I still own most of them. I have quite a collection here in Meggen.

When I was a kid, the first real flute I got was a Selmer Gold Seal, but, as I've related, it wasn't any good. I don't think it was any good when I took it out of the box, and it did not improve with my tinkering with it. I finally gave up and took it to my dad's friend Purdy Flack, who repaired instruments in the back of his house. He pronounced it hopeless and offered to sell me as a replacement a flute made by E. J. Albert in Brussels. I never knew how my dad managed to come up with the out-of-sight sum of £30, but he did, and it was a good instrument.

I played that Albert flute for the remainder of the time that I studied with Muriel Dawn and all through my first year in London. During that first year at the Royal College of Music, I made enough money playing with amateur orchestras, amateur opera groups, and the odd professional group around town to buy a new flute. That instrument—the first one that I had bought myself—was a Haynes closed-hole, offset-G, low-C flute. I know this won't mean a lot to most of my readers, but suffice it to say that although it was a very nice flute for its time, which was the mid-fifties, it's a sort of flute that no serious musician would play today.

Then, suddenly, Albert Cooper emerged on the London scene. He had apprenticed and worked for years with the great London flute-making firm Rudall, Carte and Co., and in 1959 he went out on his own.

I had a connection to Cooper through my old friend William Bennett, who was a friend and collaborator of Cooper's, along with Alexander Murray, Elmer Cole, and other London flute players. Together, they came up with a method of tuning the flute that became known as the Cooper scale. This was a tremendous advance over the Boehm scale, which had revolutionized flute making a hundred years earlier. Now Cooper started a new revolution that completely changed the way flutes were made worldwide.

Haynes was about the only large flute firm that did not go in the Cooper direction. Suddenly, everyone was using Albert Cooper's scale. Some asked for his permission, which he gladly gave; others simply advertised a modified scale. If you don't play the flute yourself, this may not mean much, but I can assure you it is like night and day playing on a Cooper-scale flute compared to some of the old fashioned flutes you may encounter even now.

I was still with Sadler's Wells when I ordered my first Cooper flute—my first in-line, open-hole, low-B flute, which is what nearly all professional flute players use today. I remember Wibb Bennett taking me to Mr. Cooper's house to place the order. Mr. Cooper told it me would cost £129, so I had to scrounge a bit to find the money—as I've mentioned, we were paid £21 a week, so £129 was quite a tidy sum.

I did have an account with the Westminster Bank in Great Portland Street. I never kept a fortune in this account, but now I asked the bank for a loan. To my relief and delight, Mr. Miller, the bank manager, who had informed himself on the subject of flute making specially for my interview, agreed to lend me the £129. You may be wondering why this episode has remained in my memory all these years. There is a reason, and it is that I was the first person in the history of the Galways to have an account in a bank! As for the amount in pounds sterling, I remember this so precisely because a little while later I bought a cutting-edge hi-fi, and it was also £129. I've noticed that if you want to buy a silver flute nowadays—an in-line, open-hole, low–B silver flute—it will cost about £6,000, which is also roughly the price of a good amplifier these days.

After some time the flute arrived, and I was really pleased with it. It was a beautiful instrument, solid silver, and it was so much easier to play than my old Haynes. The only drawback was the head joint. When Mr. Cooper began to make flutes, he did not have the know-how on the head joint that later made him truly famous. So I put my Haynes head joint on it, and I played that Cooper flute with the Haynes head joint for nearly ten years. Then when I joined the Berlin Philharmonic, I needed a flute with a higher pitch, and I had Mr. Cooper build it for me. But I still used the same old head from the Haynes flute, because it suited me so well and I knew it inside out.

To digress for a moment regarding my problems with head joints: At some point my friend Rainer Lafin gave up playing in orchestras and turned to making and repairing flutes. Working with the Muramatsu company of Japan and with Albert Cooper, he developed a type of head joint that helps the flute player achieve an even tone all the way up and down the scale. And he keeps tinkering with it and improving it. In fact, the last time Rainer came here for a visit, he told me that he had a new version for me to try. I kidded him a little about that. "Rainer," I said, "do you mean you're letting me walk around with an out-of-date head joint? That is like wearing a suit from 1920." I have tried Rainer's head joints practically from the time he started to make them and have followed his progress along the way. His head joints are now used by leading orchestral players around the world.

Anyway, it was in Berlin that I started to earn some real money for the first time, because that orchestra was one of the best paid in the world. We had our regular salary from the West German government, and we doubled it with all the recordings we made with Karajan. With that money, I was able to order my first gold flute

Enjoying the garden in Meggen with my good friend and flute maker Rainer Lafin, probably talking about flutes—what else?

With the late world-famous flute maker Osamu Muramatsu. Muramatsu flutes are highly regarded, and I own a number of them.

from Albert, and I tell you, it is a fantastic instrument. It's still one of the best instruments I own. Everyone who plays it, even today, loves it. It's a pity that it has such a high pitch, because it was made for me to play in Berlin, but I'm not going to have it changed. I just live with it and love it.

A word here on gold flutes. Some people are convinced that gold makes no difference in the sound of a flute, but I disagree. Albert Cooper's gold flutes were brilliant sounding and more even in tone all up and down the scale than any other flutes I had ever played. In addition to these qualities, the lower register is more flexible and offers a greater range of tone colors. As far as I was concerned, these Cooper flutes were the best on the market, and it was the direction in flute making that I wanted to go. I have played only gold and platinum flutes ever since Mr. Cooper made me that first gold flute to play in the Berlin Philharmonic.

Incidentally, there's another reason, unrelated to the tone, why I never went back to playing silver flutes. Silver keys are not as strong as gold keys. If you're in an orchestra, this may not matter so much, but if you're touring all over the world, you really need the strongest flute you can get. You need something that will not alter or need regulating in the course of a tour.

Meanwhile, when I was with the Berlin Philharmonic, I had a student named James Fenwick Smith, who was also a flute maker. When Fenwick arrived on the Berlin scene, he said, "Try this flute." He gave me a Powell that he had made, and he said, "This is one of the best flutes in the world."

I tried it out a bit, and I said, "Well, Fenwick, this is a nice flute, but it's sort of old-fashioned in the scale that it has. Here's one of my flutes. Try this." So I gave him my silver Cooper to play.

Fenwick came back a couple of days later and said, "This is an *amazing* flute." He copied the scale of the Cooper flute and made a couple of flutes *exactly* as Mr. Cooper made them. Both of them were gold flutes. I don't remember where we got the gold, but we bought several pieces, and Fenwick worked on these two instruments. He used keys from Powell and put the flutes together with the name Powell on them. I can tell you, however, that these two flutes were actually made in Berlin, and I played them in the Berlin Philharmonic. Of course, I didn't play them all the time, because I loved my Cooper. But I never sold them, and I still have them in my collection.

When I left Berlin, I needed to get another flute, with a lower pitch. So Mr. Cooper made me a new flute, which he delivered in 1977. It was a 14-karat gold flute with a diamond embedded in the crown. (The crown is located at the end of the head joint.) How the diamond came about is that Albert was still working on this flute while I was laid up in the hospital with my two broken legs. During my convalescence, I was reading about the Crusades and how the Crusaders carried a diamond with them, if they could afford one, to ward off evil. So I got the idea of asking Albert to put a diamond in the head joint of this flute. Since then, I've been given other diamonds for my flutes, by Osamu Muramatsu and others. I don't think it changes the sound of the flute at all, but it's a bit of a conversation piece.

In any case, Mr. Cooper delivered my first diamond flute while I was still in the hospital, and as soon as I could hold it properly, I got cracking with it. That flute has served me well. There is one problem, however: these Cooper flutes are very specialized, and not everyone can fix them if something goes wrong with the pads. It's like having, say, a Ferrari—I've been told you need to have a Ferrari garage to keep it running; you can't simply take it to the mechanic around the corner. That's what Mr. Cooper's flutes were like, because he made the holes slightly smaller than other people did. Now we're talking only a fraction of a millimeter here, but the difference was enough that the average person who overhauls these flutes wouldn't have the equipment to make the pads the right size.

Meanwhile, during my many trips to Japan, starting way back with the Berlin Philharmonic, I had become friendly with some of the people at the Muramatsu firm. But I had never played their flutes because I didn't like the scale that they used. So one time when I was touring in Japan, I brought them one of my Cooper flutes, and they copied it exactly. I found this to be a very good instrument, and I could get it repaired anywhere. After that, I ordered all sorts of flutes from the Muramatsus, depending on what kind of gold they had. I gradually acquired a 9-karat gold flute, a 14-karat, an 18-karat, and a 24-karat. And, of course, platinum flutes as well. But I still love my old 14-karat Cooper, and at home I'll often pick that one up in preference to one of the newer ones.

Still, I do enjoy trying new flutes, and I believe in encouraging flute makers. So I ordered a new flute from a young American named Dana Sheridan. He made me a very fine flute, although I have to admit that I preferred the tone of my Muramatsus and my Coopers.

Then one day a colleague came to me and said, "Jimmy, I'm thinking of buying a new flute. I've got a chance to buy a gold flute." He told me who was offering it for sale.

I said, "Jonas, listen, don't buy that flute, because the person who's selling it has something better that he isn't showing you. Now, let me give you some flutes to try." I went downstairs and brought up five or six for him. When I came back after an hour, he told me that he loved the Sheridan.

"Okay, this is the deal," I said. "You can have it for a year. All you have to do is pay the insurance, and when you give it back, it has to have a complete overhaul."

A year rolled by, and I didn't hear anything from Jonas. A couple of months later, I called him and asked, "Hey, listen, what about that flute?"

He said, "Jimmy, I just haven't found a flute as good as this. I'm absolutely in love with it."

"Okay," I said. "I'm getting a flute made by Johan Brögger in Denmark. I tell you what: you pay for that flute, and you can keep the Sheridan." Because, give or take a couple of hundred Swiss francs, they were about the same price.

So that's what he did, and I got the one from Brögger, which is a fantastic flute, too. I quite often play that one in concert.

In fact, it's sometimes very difficult for me to decide which flute to play, because I've got so many really good ones. It's like having a garage full of top-of-the-line cars—you don't know which one to drive next. Do you want to use the Rolls-Royce today or the Bentley? The Maserati or the Ferrari?

One day when I was in Boston, I met a young man named Emanuel Arista. He sent me a flute, and I tried it and bought it. Eventually, however, I had to send it back to him, because he had used the scale known as the William Bennett scale, and I personally could not play it at all. Even though Wibb Bennett had worked with Albert Cooper, his scale is different from the Cooper scale, and I could not get it to work for me, the way I play the flute. So Emanuel said he would make me one with the Cooper scale. Two years rolled on, and there was no flute, so I called him up and threatened him with all sorts of things. Finally, he made the flute and brought it over. It's a *beautiful* flute, and I keep it here in Meggen among all my other flutes. In fact, except for the Sheridan, I don't believe I have ever sold a flute—although I did lose five gold flutes once when someone stole them from me at the Lucerne railroad station.

To date, I've got fifteen gold flutes, three platinum flutes, several wooden flutes, a bunch of piccolos, and two alto flutes—one is gold and the other is silver. I also have a bass flute, a contrabass flute, and a subcontrabass flute: I bought them specially for people to play in my band—that is, the orchestra we put together for the end of our master class each year. You should see all these instruments—there is more piping here than in any plumber's shop.

My favorite flute maker today is a man named Kanichi Nagahara. Kanichi is Japanese, although he has lived in the United States for many years. He is the CEO and head of his workshop, which he founded in 1991 just outside Boston. His employees are all Americans, and they are all very fine flute makers.

I own instruments other than flutes. Here I am with my alphorn, most appropriate in the majestic Swiss Alps.

Kanichi not only produces great instruments, but he also has provided me with better service than any other flute maker I have ever been involved with. He has often traveled several hundred miles just to adjust the pads on my flute or to clean and oil the instrument. That is what I call good customer service.

He made a special flute for me to celebrate my seventieth birthday, and I am very proud to own and play this outstanding instrument. One great thing to be said about small flute-making companies is that they can build a flute incorporating your every wish. This is not always so with the larger companies, which have more difficulty being flexible and responding to the needs of individual flute players. I asked Kanichi to change the height of a lever, and he did it straightaway on the instrument he is making for me.

This is not to say that I no longer love all my other flutes—especially my Coopers and Muramatsus. But for me at this time, the best of them all are the flutes made by Kanichi Nagahara.

Twenty years or so ago, I began teaching a master class in Switzerland at the request of the lady who ran the Kleintheater in Lucerne, my good friend Marianne von Allmen. Marianne booked a room in the casino, and to our amazement 60 people turned up. This led us to establish an annual weeklong class in Weggis, a little town along the lake near Vitznau. We rented space in the local school, and the first class was a runaway success, with about 150 people attending. Since then, it has leveled out at about 80 or so.

In this class, I start off the day by having a professional singer, Nina Amon, in to teach us how to sing. After all, if the flute is said to be the instrument nearest to the human voice, then we should all learn how to sing, at least at a basic level.

After we have had some instruction in singing, I show the students how to apply what we have just learned to the real art of flute

Jeanne and I look forward to our master class every summer in Switzerland.
Here we are leading the troops in Interlaken in 2006.

Me at a master class in Bern, Switzerland, some years ago.

playing. This centers on tone production, articulation, flexibility of the lips, and projection.

We then spend some time on scales and general finger technique.

This is followed by one-on-one lessons with the active participants. (We also accept a number of auditors each year.) In addition, I have a question-and-answer session that all the students attend, so that we can clear up any misunderstandings that might arise.

Meanwhile, Jeanne gives lessons in the afternoons for auditors who think they can benefit from a private session. Sometimes she comes across a talented child or adult she thinks I should hear, and we always make room in my class for such a gifted person.

Class ends at 5:30 p.m. each day, and then at 5:45 we have a flute choir, in which everyone plays. In the evenings we have one-hour recitals given by some very famous players.

After a week of singing and playing and listening to first-rate professionals, I notice a great difference in the students' playing.

The main thing we seek to instill in this class is how to practice and get the best results from what you have learned. I am sure there are many people reading this book who aren't musicians but who play golf or chess, for example, and who are only too aware that knowing how it should be done is one thing, and practicing to become a master is quite another thing.

This class is very important to me. I feel I should give back something to the upcoming generation, in recognition of all those good people who helped make the path an easier one for me to travel. I hope they will get as much fun out of it all as I have had over the last sixty-four years.

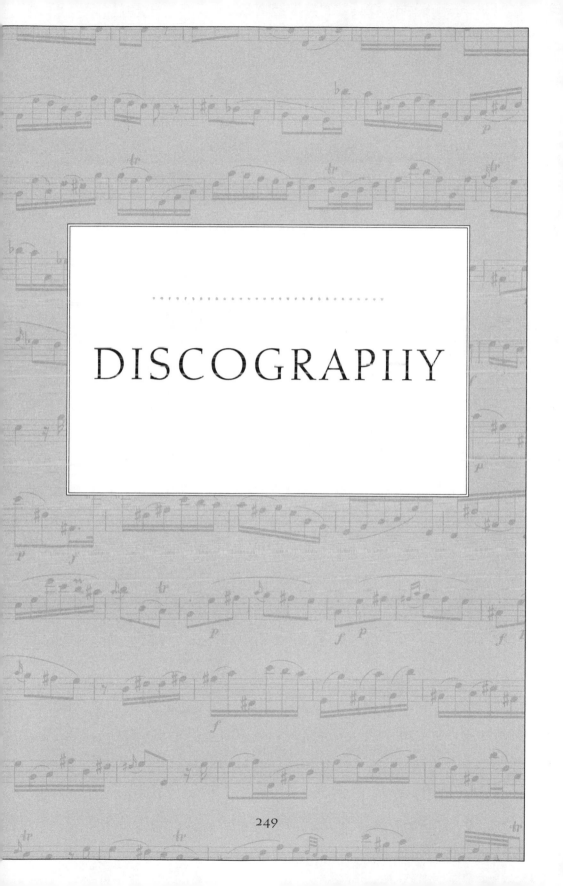

DISCOGRAPHY

All recordings are on RCA Victor Red Seal or RCA Victor unless otherwise noted.

Single-Composer Recordings

Sir Malcolm Arnold 688-60-2 (BMG Classics)
  Flute Concerto no. 2, op. 111
  Three Shanties for Wind Quintet, op. 4
  Sonatina for Flute and Piano, op. 19
  Concerto for Flute and Strings, op. 45
  Fantasy for Flute, op. 89
  Divertimento for Flute, Oboe, and Clarinet, op. 37
  Sonata for Flute and Piano, op. 121
  (Phillip Moll, piano; Gareth Hulse, oboe; Antony Pay, clarinet;
    Philip Eastop, French horn; Rachel Gough, bassoon; Sir
    Neville Marriner, conductor, Academy of St. Martin in the
    Fields)

C. P. E. Bach 60244-2-RC
  Concertos in G Major, A Major, and D Minor
  (Jörg Faerber, conductor, Württembergisches
    Kammerorchester)

J. S. Bach 62555-2
   Sonatas in B Minor, E Major, E Minor, C Major, G Minor,
      and E-flat Major
   (Phillip Moll, harpsichord; Sarah Cunningham, viola)

J. S. Bach 68182-2
   Sonatas in G Major, A Major, and C Minor from *Musical
      Offering*
   Sonata in G Major for Two Flutes and Continuo
   (Phillip Moll, harpsichord; Sarah Cunningham, viola; Monica
      Huggett, violin; Jeanne Galway, flute)

J. S. Bach 6517-2-RG
   Suite no. 2 in B Minor
   Flute Concerto in E Minor
   Trio Sonatas: no. 2 in G Major and no. 4 in C Minor
   (Kyung-Wha Chung, violin; Phillip Moll, harpsichord;
      Moray Welsh, cello; I Solisti di Zagreb)

J. S. Bach 60900-2
   Orchestral Suite no. 2
   Concerto in C Major
   Concerto for Flute, Violin, Harpsichord, and Orchestra
   (Jörg Faerber, conductor, Württembergisches
      Kammerorchester)

Beethoven 7756-2-RC
   Serenades in D Major, op. 25 and op. 8
   Flute Sonata in B-flat Major
   (Joseph Swensen, violin; Paul Neubauer, viola; Phillip Moll,
      piano)

Lennox Berkeley
   The Complete Works for Flute AGL/AGK 1-5447
   (Phillip Moll, piano; Lennox Berkeley, conductor, London
      Philharmonic)

John Corigliano 56602-2
Pied Piper Fantasy
"Voyage"
(David Effron, conductor, Eastman Philharmonia)

Franz Danzi 61673-2
Concerto for Flute and Orchestra, op. 31
Concertante for Flute, Clarinet, and Orchestra, op. 41
Fantasia for Clarinet and Orchestra on "Là ci darem la mano"
(Sabine Meyer, clarinet; Jörg Faerber, conductor,
   Württembergisches Kammerorchester)

Mauro Giuliani 60237-2
Gran Duetto Concertante in A Major
Duo Concertant in E Minor
Serenade in A Major
(Kazuhito Yamashita, guitar; Joseph Swensen, violin; Elizabeth
   Anderson, cello)

Aram Ilich Khachaturian RCD1-7010
Concerto for Flute and Orchestra
Adagio from *Spartacus*
"Masquerade Waltz"
Sabre Dance from *Gayane*
(Myung-whun Chung, conductor, Royal Philharmonic
   Orchestra)

Lowell Liebermann 63235-2
Concerto for Flute and Orchestra, op. 39
Concerto for Flute, Harp, and Orchestra, op. 48
Concerto for Piccolo and Orchestra, op. 50
(Hyun-Sun Na, harp; Lowell Liebermann, conductor,
   London Mozart Players)

· Mancini: *In the Pink* RCD1-5315
   "The Pink Panther," "Breakfast at Tiffany's," "Moon River,"
   "Pennywhistle Jig," "*The Thorn Birds* Theme," "Pie in the
   Face Polka," "Baby Elephant Walk," and other pieces
   (Henry Mancini, conductor, National Philharmonic
   Orchestra)

John Mayer RL/RK 25389
   Shri Krishna, Mandala ki Raga Sangeet
   (Hiroyuki Iwaki, conductor, London Philharmonic)

Saverio Mercadante 61447-2
   Flute Concertos in D Major, E Minor, and E Major
   (Claudio Scimone, conductor, I Solisti Veneti)

Mozart 68256-2
   Concerto no. 1 in G Major, K. 313, and no. 2 in D
      Major, K. 314
   Concerto for Flute and Harp in C Major, K. 299
   (Marisa Robles, harp; Neville Marriner, conductor, Academy
      of St. Martin in the Fields)

Mozart 7861-2-RC
   Concerto no. 1 in G Major, K. 313, and no. 2 in D Major,
      K. 314
   Andante in C Major, K. 315
   Rondo, K. 373
   Concerto for Flute and Harp in C Major, K. 299
   Menuetto from Divertimento in D Major, K. 334
   Eine kleine Nachtmusik (Serenade in G Major), K. 525
   (Marisa Robles, harp; Chamber Orchestra of Europe)

Mozart 60442-2
   Flute Quartets: K. 285, K. 285a, K. 285b, K. 298,
      and K. 370
   (Tokyo String Quartet)

Mozart 61789-2
Concerto for Flute and Harp in C Major, K. 299
Sonatas for Flute and Piano in F Major, K. 376, and in
C Major, K. 296
(Marisa Robles, harp; Phillip Moll, piano; Michael Tilson
Thomas, conductor, London Symphony Orchestra)

Mozart 6723-2-RG
Concerto no. 1 in G Major, K. 313
Andante in C Major, K. 315
(Rudolf Baumgartner, conductor, Festival Strings Lucerne)
Concerto for Flute and Harp in C Major, K. 299
(Marisa Robles, harp; Eduardo Mata, conductor, London
Symphony Orchestra)

Mozart: *My Magic Flute* 477-6233 (Deutsche Grammophon)
Concerto for Flute and Harp in C Major, K. 299
Andante from Piano Concerto no. 21 in C Major, K. 467
Theme and Variations from Piano Sonata no. 11 in A Major,
K. 331
"Ruhe sanft, mein holdes Leben" from *Zaïde*
Rondo all Turca
"The Magic Flutes" (a medley arranged by David Overton)
(Catrin Finch, harp; Jeanne Galway, flute; Sinfonia Varsovia)

Carl Nielsen 56359-2
Concerto for Flute
(Danish Radio Symphony Orchestra)
Wind Quintet
(Bjorn Fosdal, horn; Bjorn Carl Nielsen, oboe; Niels
Thomsen, clarinet; Jens Tofte-Hansen, bassoon)
Two Fantasy Pieces
(Phillip Moll, piano)
"Faith and Hope Are Playing"
(Sioned Williams, harp; Brian Hawkins, viola)

Joseph Joachim Quantz NTZ 60247-2-RC
   Concertos in G Major, C Major, G Minor, and
      D Major
   (Jörg Faerber, conductor, Württembergisches
      Kammerorchester)

Carl Heinrich Reinecke ARC/ARE 1-4584
   Sonata, op. 167, *Undine*
   Concerto in D Major, op. 283
   (Phillip Moll, piano; Hiroyuki Iwaki, conductor, London
      Philharmonic)

Rodrigo RL/RK 25193 or AGL/AGK 1-5446
   Concierto pastoral
   Fantasia para un gentilhombre
   (Eduardo Mata, conductor, Philharmonia)

Schubert 55303-2
   Arpeggione Sonata, D. 821
   Introduction and Variations on *Die schöne Müllerin*
   (Phillip Moll, piano)

Telemann ARL/ARK 1-3488
   Suite in A Minor for Flute and Strings
   Concertos in G Major and C Major
   (I Solisti di Zagreb)

Vivaldi 60748-2-RG
   The Four Seasons
   (I Solisti di Zagreb)

Vivaldi 7928-2-RC
   Six Flute Concertos: RV 436, RV 108, RV 427, RV 438, RV
      440, RV 429
   (Claudio Scimone, conductor, I Solisti Veneti)

Vivaldi 61351-2

Flute Concertos, op. 10: RV 433, RV 439, RV 428, RV 435, RV 434, RV 437

(New Irish Chamber Orchestra)

Multi-Composer Recordings

Annie's Song & Other Galway Favorites 60747-2-RG

"Liebesfreud" (Kreisler), "Berceuse" (Fauré), "Annie's Song" (Denver), "Brian Boru's March" (traditional Irish), "*Carmen* Fantasy" (Bizet), and other pieces

(Charles Gerhardt, conductor, National Philharmonic Orchestra)

At the Movies 61326 2

"Moon River," "The Way We Were," "Never on Sunday," "I Will Wait for You," "Over the Rainbow," and other film tunes

(Vincent Fanuele, Julian Lee, Jonathan Tunick, and Jeff Berger, conductors, Galway Pops Orchestra)

The Celtic Minstrel 68393-2

"I'll Take You Home Again, Kathleen," "The Minstrel Boy," "I Dreamed I Dwelt in Marble Halls," "Cath chéim an fhia" ("The Battle of Deer's Leap"), and other Irish songs

(Emily Mitchell, harp; the Chieftains)

Christmas Carol 61233-2

Chorale from the *Christmas Oratorio* (Bach), "I Wonder as I Wander" (traditional American), "Sheep May Safely Graze" (Bach), "Jesus Christ the Apple Tree" (Poston), "We Wish You a Merry Christmas" (Warrell, Ryan), and other songs for Christmas

(John Birch, organ; BBC Singers; Royal Philharmonic Orchestra; Chapel Choir of King's School, Canterbury)

Cleo Laine & James Galway RCD1-3628
"Sometimes When We Touch," "Play It Again, Sam,"
"Skylark," "Still Was the Night," and other songs
(Cleo Laine, soprano)

The Enchanted Forest—Melodies of Japan 7893-2-RC
"The Enchanted Forest," "Tokuyama Lullaby," "Star
Children," and other Japanese songs
(Hiro Fujikake, synthesizer)

French Flute Concertos GK 85448
Ibert: Concerto for Flute and Orchestra
Chaminade: Concertino for Flute and Orchestra,
op. 107
Poulenc: Sonata for Flute and Orchestra
Fauré: Fantaisie for Flute and Orchestra
(Charles Dutoit, conductor, Royal Philharmonic
Orchestra)

The French Recital 68351-2
Fauré: Sonata for Flute and Piano, op. 13
Widor: Suite for Flute and Piano, op. 34
Debussy: Prelude to *L'Apres-midi d'un faune*
Debussy: "La Plus que lente"
Debussy: "La Fille aux cheveux de lin"
Debussy: "En Bateau" from *Petite Suite*
(Christopher O'Riley, piano)

Hommage à Rampal 63701-2
François Devienne: Concerto no. 8 for Flute and Orchestra
in G Major
François Devienne: Concerto no. 7 for Flute and Orchestra
in E Minor
Domenico Cimarosa: Concerto for Two Flutes and Chamber
Orchestra
(Jeanne Galway, flute; London Mozart Players)

Ich War ein Berliner (Deutsche Grammophon)

Excerpts from *Peer Gynt* Suite (Grieg), *L'Arlésienne* (Bizet), Mass in B Minor (Bach), Wind Quintet in B-flat Major (Danzi), Quintet in C Major (Reicha), Serenade in D Major, K. 320 (Mozart), *Aïda* (Verdi), and *Salome* (Strauss)

(Daniel Deffayet, saxophone; Gundula Janowitz, soprano; Peter Schreier, tenor; Günter Piesk, bassoon; Lothar Koch, oboe; Karl Leister, clarinet; Gerd Seifert, horn; Karl Böhm, conductor, Berlin Philharmonic; Herbert von Karajan, conductor, Berlin Philarmonic)

Impressions 62552-2

Debussy: Quartet for Strings in G Minor

Ravel: Quartet for Strings in F Major

Ravel: Introduction and Allegro for Harp, Flute, Clarinet, and String Quartet

(Heidi Lehwalder, harp; Richard Stoltzman, clarinet; Tokyo String Quartet)

In Dulci Jubilo 60736-2-RC

"O Tannenbaum," "Adeste Fideles," "Ave Maria" (Bach-Gounod), "In Dulci Jubilo," "Jesu, Joy of Man's Desiring," "Stille Nacht, heilige Nacht," and other songs for Christmas

(John Georgiadis, conductor, Regensburger Domspatzen and Munich Radio Symphony Orchestra)

Italian Flute Concertos 61164-2

Giovanni Battista Pergolesi: Concerto in G

Baldassare Galuppi: Concerto in D

Romano Antonio Piacentino: Concerto in G

Louis Gianella: *Concerto Lugubre*

Giuseppe Tartini: Concerto in G

(Claudio Scimone, conductor, I Solisti Veneti)

Italian Serenade 61148-2
  Giuliani: Gran Duetto Concertante
  Galway and Yamashita (after Cimarosa): Serenade
  Paganini: Sonata concertata
  Rossini: Andante and Variations on "Di tanti palpiti"
  Bazzini: "La Ronde des Lutins"
  (Kazuhito Yamashita, guitar)

James Galway and the Chieftains in Ireland 5798-2-RC
  "Danny Boy," "Down by the Salley Gardens," "Give Me
    Your Hand," "She Moved through the Fair," "Tristan and
    Isolde," and other Irish songs

James Galway & Martha Argerich: Sonatas for Flute and Piano 5095
  Franck: Sonata in A
  Prokofiev: Sonata in D
  (Martha Argerich, piano)

James Galway and Phillip Moll Play Dvořák–Feld–Martinu 57802-2
  Antonín Dvořák: Sonatina for Violin and Piano in
    G Major, op. 100
  Jindrich Feld: Sonata for Flute and Piano
  Bohuslav Martinu: Sonata for Flute and Piano
  (Phillip Moll, piano)

James Galway Plays Stamitz RL/RK 24315
  Johann Stamitz: Concertos in D Major and G Major
  C. P. E. Bach: Unaccompanied Sonata in A Minor
  (André Prieur, conductor, New Irish Chamber Orchestra)

The Lark in the Clear Air 61379-2
  "The Lark in the Clear Air" (traditional English), Adagio
    (Albinoni), "Gymnopédie no. 1" (Satie), "Notturno" from
    String Quartet no. 2 (Borodin), "The Swan" (Saint-Saëns),
    "Last Spring" (Grieg), Adagio from String Quartet op. 11
    (Barber), and other pieces
  (Hiro Fujikake, synthesizer)

Legends 68776-2
  "Danny Boy," "Riverdance," "Lanigan's Ball," "Lament for the
    Wild Geese," "Hoe Down," and other Irish songs
  (Phil Coulter, piano)

Man with the Golden Flute 60924-2
  "Moto Perpetuo" (Paganini), "The Flight of the Bumblebee"
    (Rimsky-Korsakov), "Minute Waltz" (Chopin), "The
    Dance of the Blessed Spirits" (Glück), and other pieces
  (Charles Gerhardt, conductor, National Philharmonic Orchestra)

Music for My Friends 68882-2
  Nocturne et Allegro scherzando (Gaubert), "Il carnevale di
    Venezia" (Briccialdi), Andante et Rondo, op. 25 (Doppler),
    Fantaisie (Hüe), Concertino for Flute and Piano, op. 107
    (Chaminade), and other pieces
  (Phillip Moll, piano; Jeanne Galway, flute)

Music for My Little Friends 63725-2
  "Rondo alla Turca" (Mozart), "Lament for the Wild Geese"
    (Coulter), "The Little White Donkey" (Ibert), "Madrigal"
    (Gaubert), and other pieces
  (Phillip Moll, piano; London Mozart Players)

O'Reilly Street 1 DW09NM (Sony BMG/Red Seal)
  Claude Bolling: Suite for Flute and Jazz Piano Trio
  Jorge Gomez: "Espiegle General O'Reilly," "Tica-Tica,"
    "Soncito," and "Contradanza"
  Bach: Badinerie from Orchestral Suite no. 2 in B minor for
    Flute and Strings
  (Jorge Gomez, piano; Tiempo Libre)

Over the Sea to Skye—The Celtic Collection 60424-2-RC
  "O'Carolan's Quarrel with the Landlady," "The Rowan
    Tree," "A Slip and Double Jig," "Cath chéim an fhia,"
    "Lillibulero," and other traditional songs
  (The Chieftains)

Phoenix AGL/AGK 1-5450
   John Carmichael: *Phoenix* Concerto for Flute and
      Orchestra
   Clifford Abbott: Flute Concerto
   Arthur Benjamin: "Jamaican Rumba"
   (Louis Frémaux and David Measham, conductors, Sydney
      Symphony Orchestra)

Quiet on the Set: James Galway at the Movies 50932-2
   Music from the movies, including the themes from *The Horse
      Whisperer*, *Forrest Gump*, and *Braveheart*
   (Jeanne Galway, flute; London Mozart Players)

A Song of Home: An American Musical Journey 6388325
   "My Cape Breton Home," "I Dream of Jeannie," "The West
      Texas Waltz," "Presidential Hornpipes," "Amazing Grace,"
      and other tunes
   (Jay Ungar, fiddle; Molly Mason, guitar and voice; Peter
      Ostroushko, mandolin; Steve Rust, bass; Michael Merenda,
      guitar)

Song of the Seashore RCD1-3534
   "The Evening Primrose," "Song of the Seashell," "Sunlight
      Shining through the Trees," "The Moon on the Ruined
      Castle," "Song of the Seashore," and other Japanese songs
   (Hiroyuki Iwaki, conductor, Tokyo String Orchestra)

Tango del Fuego 63422-2
   "The Girl from Ipanema," "Corcovado," "Tango del Fuego,"
      and other Latin jazz tunes

Un-Break My Heart 1T3H9 (BMG Classics)
   "Can You Feel the Love Tonight?," "Un-Break My Heart,"
      "Time to Say Good-bye," "Isn't She Lovely," and other
      songs by Elton John, Willie Nelson, and others
   (Mike Mower, piano)

The Wayward Wind RCD1-4222
 "Don't It Make My Brown Eyes Blue," "Duelin' Banjos,"
 "Shenandoah," "Montana Skies," "The Wayward Wind,"
 and other American songs

The Wind beneath My Wings 60862-2-RC
 "Unchained Melody," "La Vie en rose," "Smoke Gets in
 Your Eyes," "The Windmills of Your Mind," "Send in the
 Clowns," and other popular songs
 (Vincent Fanuele, conductor, Galway Pops Orchestra)

Wind of Change 62700-2
 "Here, There and Everywhere," "Tears in Heaven," "A Whole
 New World," "When a Man Loves a Woman," and other
 songs by John Lennon, Paul McCartney, Elton John, Dolly
 Parton, Stevie Wonder, and others
 (Jeanne Galway, flute; George Galway, saxophone)

Wings of Song 477508-5 (Deutsche Grammophon)
 "Pavane pour une enfante defunte" (Ravel), "Ave Maria"
 (Schubert), "En Aranjuez" (Rodrigo), "Casta diva"
 (Bellini), "Pie Jesu" (Fauré), Barcarolle (Offenbach),
 "Wesendonk Lieder" (Wagner), "Wiegenlied" (Brahms),
 "*Lord of the Rings* Suite" (Shore), "Annie's Song" (Denver),
 and other pieces
 (Moray Welsh, cello; Jeanne Galway, flute; Klauspeter Seibel,
 conductor, London Symphony Orchestra)

Winter's Crossing 32452
 "Farewell to County Antrim," "Thousands Are Sailing,"
 "Cailin na gruaige baine," "Winter's Crossing," "Grand
 Banks Newfoundland," and other songs about the emigra-
 tion from Northern Ireland to America
 (Phil Coulter, piano; Liam Neeson, narrator; Irish
 Philharmonia)

Collections

The Classical James Galway 57011-2
  Vivaldi: Concerto op. 10, no. 3 ("Il Gardellino")
  J. S. Bach: Concerto in A Minor
  C. P. E. Bach: Sonata in A Minor
  Handel: "Arrival of the Queen of Sheba" from *Solomon*
  J. S. Bach: Trio Sonata no. 3 in G Major
  John Field: Nocturne no. 5 in B-flat Major
  Telemann: Concerto in G
  Schubert: Serenade
  Mozart: Andante in C, K. 315
  (Phillip Moll, harpsichord; Kyung-Wha Chung, violin;
    Moray Welsh, cello; New Irish Chamber Orchestra; I
    Solisti di Zagreb; Chamber Orchestra Europe; David
    Measham, conductor, National Philharmonic Orchestra;
    Rudolf Baumgartner, conductor, Festival Strings Lucerne)

The Concerto Collection 60450-2-RC (4 CDs)
  Concertos by Bach, Vivaldi, Stamitz, Mozart, Mercadante,
    Reinecke, Mayer, Rodrigo, Khachaturian, Ibert, and Nielsen
  (I Solisti di Zagreb; New Irish Chamber Orchestra; Sir
    Neville Marriner, conductor, Academy of St. Martin in the
    Fields; Danish Radio Symphony Orchestra; I Solisti Veneti;
    Hiroyuki Iwaki, conductor, Tokyo String Orchestra; Eduardo
    Mata, conductor, London Symphony Orchestra; Myung-
    whun Chung, conductor, Royal Philharmonic Orchestra;
    Charles Dutoit, conductor, Royal Philharmonic Orchestra)

Dances for Flute 60917-2/4
  Waltz from Suite of Three Pieces (Godard), Waltz in D-flat
    (Chopin), "Crowley's Reel" (traditional Irish), "Pie in the
    Face Polka" (Mancini), Jamaican Rumba (Benjamin),
    Tambourin (Gossec), "Schön Rosmarin" (Kreisler), and
    other pieces

(Charles Gerhardt, conductor, National Philharmonic
Orchestra; Myung-whun Chung, conductor, Royal
Philharmonic Orchestra; Claudio Scimone, conductor,
I Solisti Veneti; Henry Mancini, conductor, National
Philharmonic Orchestra; and others)

The Essential James Galway 7431-13385-2
Works by Debussy, Denver, Khachaturian, Massenet, Rimsky-
Korsakov, Sondheim, and others
(Marisa Robles, harp; Phillip Moll, piano; Graham
Oppenheimer, viola; John Georgiadis, conductor, Munich
Radio Orchestra; Myung-whun Chung, conductor, Royal
Philharmonic Orchestra; David Measham, conductor,
National Philharmonic Orchestra; Charles Gerhardt, con-
ductor, National Philharmonic Orchestra; and Sir Neville
Marriner, conductor, Academy of St. Martin in the Fields)

Flute Sonatas 61615-2 (BMG Classics)
Franck: Sonata in A
Prokofiev: Sonata in D
(Martha Argerich, piano)
Reinecke: Sonata, op. 167, *Undine*
(Phillip Moll, piano)

James Galway's Greatest Hits, Vol. 1 7778-2-RC
"The Pink Panther" (Mancini), "Angel of Music"
(Lloyd Webber), "Clair de lune" (Debussy), "Danny Boy"
(traditional Irish), "Annie's Song" (Denver),
"The Flight of the Bumblebee" (Rimsky-Korsakov),
"Greensleeves" (Henry VIII), Canon in D (Pachelbel),
"Brian Boru's March" (traditional Irish), and
other pieces
(The Chieftains; Henry Mancini, conductor, National
Philharmonic Orchestra; Charles Gerhardt, conductor,
National Philharmonic Orchestra; and others)

James Galway's Greatest Hits, Vol. 2 61178-2
"Zui Zui Zukkorobashi" (traditional Japanese), "Jesu, Joy of
Man's Desiring" (Bach), "The Fluter's Ball" (traditional
French), "Molly on the Shore" (Grainger), "Something for
the Leprechaun" (Mancini), and other songs
(Cleo Laine, soprano; Marisa Robles, harp; Graham
Oppenheimer, viola; the Chieftains; Vincent Fanuele,
conductor, Galway Pops Orchestra; Henry Mancini, con-
ductor, National Philharmonic Orchestra)

James Galway's Greatest Hits, Vol. 3 63110-2
"Riverdance," "The Minstrel Boy," "Song of the Seashell,"
theme from *Beauty and the Beast*, and other tunes
(The Chieftains; Phil Coulter, piano)

James Galway—A Portrait 68412-2
"The Flight of the Bumblebee" (Rimsky-Korsakov),
"Carnival in Venice" (Briccialdi), Allegro from Flute
Concerto in D Major (Mozart) "Berceuse" (Fauré),
Minuet and Badinerie from Orchestral Suite no. 2 (Bach),
"Danny Boy" (traditional Irish), Rondo from *Concierto pas-
toral* (Rodrigo), "Waltzing Matilda" (traditional Australian),
and other works; plus a CD-ROM with photos and
narration
(Charles Gerhardt, conductor, National Philharmonic
Orchestra; I Solisti di Zagreb; Eduardo Mata, conductor,
London Symphony Orchestra; David Measham, conduc-
tor, Sydney Symphony Orchestra)

Love Song
"I Will Wait for You," "Unforgettable," "Can't Help Falling in
Love," "Plaisir d'amour," and other songs
(Mike Mower, piano; Hiro Fujikake, synthesizer; Vincent
Fanuele, conductor, Galway Pops Orchestra; Julian Lee,
conductor, Galway Pops Orchestra)

The Magic Flute of James Galway 60918-2

"Arrival of the Queen of Sheba" from *Solomon* (Handel), "Vocalise" (Rachmaninoff), excerpts from *A Midsummer Night's Dream* (Mendelssohn), "Träumerei" (Schumann), "Humoresque" (Dvořák), and other pieces

(Charles Gerhardt, conductor, National Philharmonic Orchestra; Myung-Whun Chung, conductor, Royal Philharmonic Orchestra)

Meditations 74321-37731-2

Adagio (Albinoni), Largo from *Xerxes* (Handel), Pastoral Symphony from *Messiah* (Handel), "Méditation" from *Thaïs* (Massenet), "The Little Shepherd" (Debussy), Nocturne no. 5 in B-flat (John Field), *Fantasia para un gentilhombre* (Rodrigo), En Bateau (Debussy), "Vocalise" (Rachmaninoff), and other works

(Marisa Robles, harp; Graham Oppenheimer, viola; Malcolm Proud, harpsichord; John Georgiadis, conductor, Munich Radio Orchestra; David Measham, conductor, National Philharmonic Orchestra; Charles Gerhardt, conductor, National Philharmonic Orchestra; Claudio Scimone, conductor, I Solisti Veneti; Jörg Faerber, conductor, Württembergisches Kammerorchester)

Pachelbel Canon and Other Baroque Favorites 61928-2

Canon in D (Pachelbel), Concerto in D Major (Vivaldi), Suite for Flute and Strings in A Minor (Telemann), Sonata in A Minor (Handel), Suite no. 3 in D Major (Bach), Concerto in C (Quantz), Le basque (Marin Marais), and other works

(Phillip Moll, harpsichord; John Birch, organ; Moray Welsh, cello; Sarah Cunningham, viola; Kyung-Wha Chung, violin; Malcolm Proud, harpsichord; Maria Graf, harp; Jörg Faerber, conductor, Württembergisches Kammerorchester; John Georgiadis, conductor, Munich Radio Orchestra; Charles

Gerhardt, conductor, National Philharmonic Orchestra;
I Solisti di Zagreb; New Irish Chamber Orchestra)

Seasons 61915-2
   "Morning" from the *Peer Gynt* Suite (Grieg), "The Last Rose of
      Summer" (Stevenson), "La Vie en rose" (Louiguy, Piaf, David),
      "Song of the Deep Forest" (Fujikake), and other works
   (Hiro Fujikake, synthesizer; Marisa Robles, harp; Emily
      Mitchell, harp; the Chieftains; RCA Victor Concert
      Orchestra; Hiroyuki Iwaki, conductor, Tokyo String
      Orchestra; David Measham, conductor, National
      Philharmonic Orchestra; Vincent Fanuele, conductor,
      Galway Pops Orchestra)

Serenade 60033-2-RC
   Serenade (Schubert), Nocturne in E-flat (Chopin), "La Fille
      aux cheveux de lin" Debussy), Concerto for Flute and
      Harp in C Major, K. 299 (Mozart), Adagio from *Spartacus*
      (Khachaturian), "Méditation" from *Thaïs* (Massenet),
      "Bachianas Brasileiras" (Villa-Lobos), "Song of the
      Seashore" (Narita), and other works
   (Phillip Moll, piano; Marisa Robles, harp; Graham
      Oppenheimer, viola; Kazuhito Yamashita, guitar; John
      Birch, organ; David Measham, conductor, National
      Philharmonic Orchestra; Charles Gerhardt, conductor,
      National Philharmonic Orchestra; Myung-whun Chung,
      conductor, Royal Philharmonic Orchestra; Barry Griffiths,
      conductor, Royal Philharmonic Orchestra)

60: Sixty Years, Sixty Flute Masterpieces Collection 760456
   (BMG Classics)
   A fifteen-CD boxed set celebrating Galway's sixtieth birth-
      day. Highlights include: Suite no. 2 in B Minor (Bach),
      Concerto in E—"Spring" (Vivaldi), "Il carnevale di
      Venezia" (Briccialdi), Sonata in A (Franck), "La flute de

Pan" (Mouquet), *Fantasia para un gentilhombre* (Rodrigo),
Three Shanties for Wind Quintet (Arnold), and Concerto
for Flute and Orchestra (Liebermann)
(Collaborators include Martha Argerich, piano; Phillip
Moll, piano; Marisa Robles, harp; Kazuhito Yamashita,
guitar; Jörg Faerber, conductor, Württembergisches
Kammerorchester; Myung-whun Chung, conductor,
Royal Philharmonic Orchestra; Lowell Liebermann, con-
ductor, London Mozart Players; and Eduardo Mata, con-
ductor, London Symphony Orchestra)

The Very Best of James Galway (two-disc set spanning
1975–1999) 68773
Selections from Pachelbel, Khachaturian, Tamezo Narita,
Massenet, Bach, Mozart, Jay Ungar, Paul Simon, Antonio
Carlos Jobim, Dolly Parton, John Denver, Andrew Lloyd
Webber, and others
(Phillip Moll, piano; Sarah Cunningham, viola; Phil Coulter,
piano; Mike Mower, flute; John Georgiadis, conductor,
Munich Radio Orchestra; Myung-whun Chung, con-
ductor, Royal Philharmonic Orchestra; Hiroyuki Iwaki,
conductor, Tokyo String Orchestra; David Measham,
conductor, National Philharmonic Orchestra; Charles
Gerhardt, conductor, National Philharmonic Orchestra;
Sir Neville Marriner, conductor, Academy of St. Martin
in the Fields; Vincent Fanuele, conductor, Galway Pops
Orchestra; and others)

Videos

Concerto! VHS 61783
Mozart: Concerto for Flute and Harp in C Major, K. 299
(Marisa Robles, harp; Michael Tilson Thomas, conductor,
London Symphony Orchestra; introduction and interview
by Dudley Moore)

James Galway and The Chieftains in Ireland VHS 60751; DVD
"Danny Boy," "Down by the Salley Gardens," "Give Me
Your Hand," "She Moved through the Fair," "Tristan and
Isolde," and other Irish songs

James Galway at 50 Laser/VHS 60572
Storytelling; scenes from a master class; a visit from old friend
Billy Dunwoody; rehearsal and performance with Claudio
Scimone and I Solisti Veneti in Innsbruck

James Galway's Christmas Carol Laser/VHS 60572
Boys of St. Alban's Cathedral Choir; the Ambrosian Singers;
Royal Philharmonic Orchestra

Peace on Earth: A Bavarian Christmas Laser/VHS 61367
Bach: Sonatas for Flute and Keyboard in C Major and E-flat
Major, BWV 1033
(Maria Graf, harp; Enoch zu Guttenberg and Dr. Stefan
Mikorey, conductors, Bamberg Symphony Orchestra)

Vivaldi: Concerti for Flute 280WC4M (Hardy Classics DVD)
Six Flute Concertos, op. 10
Concerto in C Major for Two Flutes and Orchestra
(Jeanne Galway, flute; Claudio Scimone, conductor, I Solisti
Veneti; filmed at the Palazzo Ducale, Venice)

Index